What People Are

The Change in Us

Miracles of the heart are some of the most powerful miracles on earth! If you have any doubt of the miraculous power of Jesus Christ, you must pick up this book and read it from cover to cover! I had trouble putting it down as I read through the pages of Heather's journey. We are not promised a pain-free life. Heather is living proof that God specializes in making a supernatural pathway through the sea of trouble and sorrow. It is so beautiful to see the thread of God's love weaving through Heathers life. God never forces us, but his extended hand of love is always there.

—Christy Christopher,
Christian author and speaker

Wow . . . just *wow*! I don't have words really. It's a page turner. I'm confident I've never read any other book in one day! It's so easy to read and follow! Heather is so vulnerable and transparent in this emotionally moving and powerful book! What an accomplishment and achievement! All my words would fall short of what I want to express. I'm sure the Lord is whispering, "Well done, good and faithful servant." This story needed to be told and God will use it for His glory!

—Kenny Morgan,
Pastor, Olive Tree Christian Fellowship Church

Heather Stover has effectively introduced herself to us by writing a powerful memoir of God's redeeming love and His relentless pursuit of His children! From the depths of emotional hurt and heartache as a child, to the traumatic physical and psychological pain as a young wife and mother, Heather chronicles the incredible work of Christ that has completely transformed her life and that of her family. Each chapter takes the reader on an unexpected turn as Heather discloses her journey with great transparency and vulnerability, yet like all good stories, she adeptly weaves together each experience for a full and rich picture of God's plan. I was reminded time and again upon reading, that we often have no idea what stories lie behind the eyes of our friends, colleagues, and neighbors. *The Change in Us* is not only the remarkable reflections of a changed woman, but a touching reminder of just how much our heavenly Father loves us.

—Dr. Cy J. Smith,
Superintendent, Mansfield Christian School

Heather Stover's story is one of overcoming abuse, addiction, illness, and a hard marriage. So much. But Heather found God in the midst of her heartache. Heather trusted God in the midst of terrible circumstances. This book will ignite your faith and remind you that God is bigger than all, of our circumstances.

—Mary R. Snyder,
Author/Speaker

Heather Stover takes readers on an emotionally transparent journey down the winding roads of family, addiction, music, healing, and reconciliation. A must-read book for those who feel there's no light at the end of the tunnel.

—Kassie Wilson,
of GOLDPINE

You know you're in the presence of a great book when you find yourself in tears at the Introduction! Many of us experience some, kind of pain in life, but not all of us heal well. This book reminded me that God is *still* interested, He *still* redeems, He *still* restores, and He *still* loves, despite how broken we feel! Thank you for stepping out in faith to remind us that our Heavenly Father isn't the one who changes, rather He's changing us!

—Clayton Hershner,
Worship/Young Adult Minister, Mt. Gilead Church of Christ

Pursuing Jesus is so often talked about by many preachers, teachers, and authors. What is not talked about enough is Jesus, the Creator of everything, and how He pursues us. Heather talks about how God pursued her. God chased her. God was with her time and time again. He showed up. God of the universe watched over her through trials, heartaches, and mistakes, time and time again. God still pursued Heather. I just love how Heather takes us deep into what most people would think was a doomed-from-the-start story. God prevailed time and time again until Heather realized she needed Him and He wanted her. This book is encouraging and motivating. Heather shares her amazing life story and testimony about not only how God can change anyone's life, but how He deeply wants to!

—Brittany Humble
Author and Owner of B.E. Humble Clothing

The Change in Us

HEATHER N. STOVER

The Change in Us

A Story of God's
Healing Power

REDEMPTION
PRESS

The author has tried to recreate events, locales, and conversations from her memories of them. In order to maintain their anonymity, in some instances she has changed the names of individuals and may have changed some identifying characteristics and details, such as physical properties, occupations, and places of residence.

ISBN 13: 978-1-64645-536-2 (Paperback)
        978-1-64645-535-5 (ePub)
        978-1-64645-534-8 (Mobi)
LCCN: 2022906199

All glory be to God.
Thank You, Lord, for saving me.
*I love the Lord, for he heard my voice; he heard
my cry for mercy. Because he turned his ear to
me, I will call on him as long as I live.*
Psalm 116:1–2 NIV

Contents

Introduction

I have talked about writing this book since 2006.

This idea came shortly after I was married that June and learned I was expecting my first child in November of the same year. I was only twenty-two and was still dealing with a freshly shattered heart after experiencing a tragedy the year before. The new life forming in my body sparked conversations between my husband, Jayson, and me. Conversations that I would rather have avoided.

For the first time since we met three years before, we began talking about family and parents and childhood. Jayson knew very little about my past. I had chosen not to talk about it because it was too painful to remember. But as my belly grew, and along with it my excitement for this new baby, so did my fear about parenting an actual living human being.

As Jay and I talked and dreamed about the future, I began imagining the type of parents we would be—except I couldn't stay focused on who I wanted to be. Instead, my thoughts kept drifting to the parent I *didn't* want to be. As I recalled my own childhood and the only example of parents I knew, I grew sad and angry. Each conversation with my husband brought up more painful memories that I had tried so hard to forget. Each new memory brought the truth of my past closer to the surface.

Jayson and I took daily strolls around the block of our first home, and one mile-long story at a time, I revealed to him the ugliness that I had once lived. As I recounted these stories, brokenness seeped out of the cage that held my tongue. Tears that seemed to be old and stale surprised me as they bubbled up in the corners of my eyes. One day at a time, our walks brought out more hurt I hadn't known I'd buried. Each conversation revealed more unforgiveness I had been harboring, and each one felt like ripping a bandage off a deep wound.

The more I brought to the surface, the more I wanted to cram back down. I didn't know how to deal with these memories and hurts. All I knew was that when I talked about them, they hurt all over again. And I realized I wasn't okay.

While Jay was consoling and understanding, he couldn't help me, yet the more I shared with him, the more he insisted that I should write a book about my life. The idea both interested and excited me, but I knew deep down I wasn't ready to write my story. If I had chosen to write my story in 2006 when the idea first arose, it wouldn't have been complete. Though I was married and starting a family and felt happier, I still needed to deal with my past. I still needed to forgive the people in my life who had hurt me.

Life went on, and time flew by. As I began dealing with those past circumstances, I began to grow and change, and the way I thought about the book idea grew and changed too.

How? I began a relationship with the One who models parenting perfectly. The One who caused my heart to wonder and search for answers as I finally dealt with the events of my childhood. The One who was pursuing me, wanting me to come to Him for help. The One I was learning to know as God, my heavenly Father.

In November 2019, thirteen years after Jay first mentioned the idea of a book, God came to me in a dream. In my dream that night, a book appeared with the title *The Change in Us* written on the cover. The image was so clear and continued to get bigger and bigger as the dream went on. Although I don't remember hearing any audible voice in the dream, the words *It's time; make time,* played over and over in my mind.

That night in the dream, I not only received a clear vision of the title of the book, but I was also reassured that the content I had gathered from life experiences was now sufficient.

When I woke up, I couldn't shake the dream. I knew it was from God, as I felt such a strong conviction that He had given me the go-ahead for the project that had been discussed years before. I knew in my heart He had commanded that it was time to write my story.

When I told Jayson about the dream, he immediately replied, "You better get to work."

I felt the pressure growing within as it became evident that this had to happen, I had to write this book. I didn't even own a computer at that time, but on December 25, 2019, a laptop lay under our Christmas tree for me, from Jayson. I knew it was time and that I had to be obedient. I didn't know where to begin, but I had faith God would guide me.

I had no idea what I was doing, but I started writing anyway. I wasn't prepared for what was to come. The more I wrote, the more I remembered, and the more I remembered, the more I hurt. I wrote story after story, and each memory felt like it would rip apart my insides. I found myself submerged in puddles of tears and sweat as I acknowledged the hurt dwelling in my soul. Every writing session left me utterly exhausted.

The process was long and hard, but God had a plan in all of it. In fact, God had had a plan for me from the time He knit me together in my mother's womb. And through my story, He would prove the change that can come from knowing and trusting in Him for healing.

If I hadn't experienced all the hurt and brokenness of my childhood, I wouldn't have had the opportunity to heal and grow close to my only true Father, the only One who was fully capable of helping me get past my past.

PART ONE

Looking Back

For you created my inmost being;
you knit me together in my mother's womb . . .
Your eyes saw my unformed body;
all the days ordained for me were written
in your book before one of them came to be.
Psalm 139:13, 16 NIV

Chapter One

Memories

I was twelve years old. Like most nights, this one had ended in fighting and abuse, with fear crippling every inch of my small body. I ran to my room and waited until everyone was asleep. Eventually, all I could hear was the loud, bearlike snore coming from my dad. The familiar sound assured me he was not a current threat.

I lay in my bed, waiting for the voice in my head to come as it always did. This voice had made itself known when I was a very small child, and only I could hear it. I could never make sense of the noise within or figure out who it was or where it dwelled, but the longer it stayed with me, the more uncomfortable I became. The voice sounded like an echo that would at times drive me crazy. It tormented me and often made me worry that there was something very wrong with me.

"Hey, hey, *hey* . . ." it would say, a long murmuring echo

behind each word. It was there when things got quiet, but it became deafening when my dad focused his angry screaming in my direction.

My dad was a large man. Everything about him was large, from his hands to his big belly. His giant voice was just too much, and the louder he yelled at me, the louder the voice in my head became, as if it were trying to overpower the monster already attacking.

I kept a boombox on the corner of my bed, and I'd wear headphones to drown out the voice in my head. But this night, the house was silent, and for a moment, so was the noise within.

Once I was certain that everyone had fallen asleep, I tip-toed past my parents' bedroom and into the bathroom. I closed the door behind me and turned the shiny diamond-like door-knob as slowly and quietly as I could. Then I faced the mirror and stared at my reflection.

I glared at my pale, scrawny frame. The only color on my body was from my strawberry hair and new brown freckles that had just begun to appear on the bridge of my nose. My focus then turned to nothing other than my own blue eyes glaring back at me. I stared and stared until the blue was gone and all I could see was the black.

This wasn't the first time I'd noticed something in my eyes. I had always found more than myself there, and whatever it was frightened me. I had known for years that if I stared long enough, I would find more, and sometimes I did this just to make sure it was still there. The eyes that looked back at me that night were deep, dark holes of anger and the presence of something more than myself.

I focused on the bathroom mirror until I became convinced that the reflection was not me but a demon. I didn't know much about God and Satan as a child, but I knew enough from scary movies, and the torment I was living, that there was a difference between good and evil. And I felt evil present in my body.

Shaking in fear, I opened the medicine cabinet and decided that I should go ahead with my plan and swallow a bottle of aspirin. I sat down on the floor and unscrewed the childproof lid. My intention was to escape the lie that my family was living. The lie that everyone outside our house believed to be true—that we were a normal family of four who loved one another and enjoyed our time together. In truth, the abuse that ruled my life where I should have found comfort was wrecking my soul.

I poured the pills into the palm of my hand and began to cry a hard, stomach-crunching silent cry, as if I were mourning my own death. I imagined my mom and dad finding me the next morning, their tears dripping into the same puddle that mine were currently forming. I imagined my dad cradling me in his arms, his heart aching for his little girl to come back to life. I cried even harder at that thought, because every bone in my body longed for him to cradle me in his arms while I was alive. But that had always just been a far-off dream. His hands had only ever hurt me, and his words had only ever pierced my heart, leaving wounds too deep to see. I felt I had no other choice but to end my life.

I hated my life. I had been in this same tiny house with these same people for twelve years, and nothing ever improved; it only got worse. Dad's drinking was getting worse, the fights were more frequent, and the abuse hurt more and more. Mom, though she tried, couldn't be there for my brother and me like she wanted to because she, too, lived in constant fear.

My mom, older brother, and I lived in a state of fear of my

dad. I can't speak for them, but as a child, I felt real hatred toward him. I hated him for hitting us and calling us names. I hated him for his habits. I hated him for driving me to school hungover and vomiting out the truck door where my class-mates would have to cross. I hated him for not coming to my ball games and for ruining birthdays. I hated him for never hugging me.

Most of all, admittedly, I despised him for not loving me.

My brother and I spent most of our days with babysitters. Mom dropped us off on her way to work, way before the sit-ter's own children were even out of bed. When school was out, we'd ride a bus back to their house, where we'd stay until bed-time. We would have preferred to be home after school, but with Mom working long hours to make up for the habits in the home and Dad choosing to go to the bar after work instead of picking us up, this became our life.

When I was old enough to realize that by the time school let out, Dad was sitting at the bar, I grew angry and confused. Why didn't he want us?

The older I got, the more I understood what was going on. I not only hated my dad, but I began to resent my mom for allowing the hurt to happen. I pleaded with her to leave him. I know that's not something a child normally desires, but I did.

Except Mom didn't believe in divorce. A short search of scripture had led her to some guidelines that she did not fully understand.

> Therefore, what God has joined to-gether, let no one separate.
> Mark 10:9 NIV

And so she stayed. And we stayed. And life only got worse.

So there I was, sitting on that bathroom floor, imagining the beauti-ful moment when my parents would scoop me up and want nothing more than for me to open my eyes.

I put the pills in my mouth, and time stood still. Clearly, at age twelve, I knew right from wrong, and I knew this was not the right thing to do. But I so badly wanted some sort of attention from someone, anyone, who would just take the time to care about me.

I let myself daydream for another minute or two, then I spit the pills into the toilet and tiptoed back to my room. Feeling weak and helpless, I climbed into bed, still crying, and pulled on my headphones to prepare for that maddening echo that I could always count on.

As the years passed and the abuse worsened, I became more confused with life and wondered why I even existed. There were many times when I would run to my room after a session of physical and verbal abuse from my dad to see if he had left any noticeable marks on my flesh. Sometimes I would find red marks; other times there was bruising.

But nothing I saw on the surface even remotely compared to the wounds I felt on the inside. Those wounds built up, then were left open and unhealed. The fingerprints from my dad's enormous fingers would begin to fade, and I'd find myself punching them. As I watched the evidence from the slaps start to disappear, I'd try to bring them back with my own hands. I'd punch my flesh, then punch again, harder, hoping there would be a lasting bruise so someone might ask, and I could tell.

But no matter how badly I wanted someone to notice, I could never leave enough traces of the battle on the outside to spark any questions from anyone else about the battle going on inside. I needed someone to see I was hurting. I yearned for someone to notice how damaged I had become. But no one did.

The life that I had grown used to was breaking me and

sending me into a spiral of confusion and soon, rebellion.

I was damaged goods. My early childhood years left me angry and lost, and those emotions only escalated as I approached my teen years.

In the seventh grade, I started drinking, smoking, and doing drugs.

The first time I ever got high was when my brother, Josh, played a prank on me. He was two years older than me and had already begun experimenting with drugs. I'd grown up feeling sympathy for my brother because Dad always treated him the worst. Josh could never do anything good enough for our dad and was the most frequent target of his anger.

One day, Josh and a friend were skipping school. They made a phone call to the middle school I attended, pretending to be my dad. They informed the secretary that I needed to leave for an appointment at lunchtime. Schools were obviously different then, and signatures were not required for a student to leave.

I got the note that I was to go outside at lunchtime to meet my dad for this "appointment." Being oblivious, I obeyed.

When I walked out the front doors of the school on that beautiful spring day, I noticed my brother's black Ford Tempo on the side road. He and his friend were waiting on me. They motioned for me to come over and get in the car.

I'll admit, I was kind of excited. I remember initially thinking it was cool that my older brother had gotten me out of school to skip with him. Honestly, I was hungry and thought for sure we were going to get lunch or even ice cream. But when I got into the car, they rolled up all the windows. Then, with rap music bumping too loud to talk, we headed down the road, past the school, and on out of town.

Once we hit the wide-open country roads, my brother lit a joint.

I was only in seventh grade, but I knew about pot. I knew the smell from our living room where my dad sat with his serving-bowl-sized ashtray. It frequently wafted in through my bedroom window, too, from where Josh sat on the roof blowing the smoke into the night sky.

Josh insisted I take a hit, but I declined.

After the joint had all been inhaled, they pulled back up to the school and let me out. I wasn't worried as I walked back in, thinking I hadn't done anything wrong. But I was unaware of what a "contact buzz" was, or that I had gotten one. The boys had known exactly what they were doing, and this had been entertainment for them. They knew I would get high just by being in that car.

I checked in at the office, but by the time I got my things out of my locker to go to class, I knew I wasn't feeling right. I felt like I was floating and that the halls in the school were all uphill. No matter how hard I tried, I couldn't get my mind to feel normal.

Once in my class, I immediately asked to go to the restroom. I ran to the mirror, only to find my eyes fire-red and watering. The longer I stared, the more it felt as if the black in my eyes was laughing at me.

I was scared. The tears started, and I hid myself in one of the stalls. I had never been high before. I didn't know what was going to happen or how to get these strange feelings to go away. I sat there until I could pull myself together enough to make it through the rest of the day. I knew I couldn't tell anyone. I didn't want to get in trouble, and I wasn't going to tell on my brother. Memories from the last fight between him and my dad were still fresh in my mind.

I didn't know what had started the fight that day, but I'd heard them fighting in the kitchen. By the time I made it downstairs to try to intervene, it was too late.

As I pushed through the swinging doors, I saw my dad pull a frying pan up over his head.

I screamed, "Stop!" but my voice didn't faze him.

Josh, who was half Dad's size, was pinned between him and the back door. As the pan came crashing down on Josh's skull, his eyes rolled back in his head, and he sank slowly to the floor.

Pain shot through my heart, and I felt as though I had been hit with the pan too. The look on my brother's face was of deep despair. Despite knowing the blow had hurt him, he was more crushed on the inside, and that crushed me.

Burning with anger, I screamed, "I hate you! I wish you were dead!"

This detoured Dad's anger toward me, and he chased me out of the kitchen with the pan still in his hand. I pushed the front door open and flew down the three front steps. I knew he wouldn't chase me outside. The abuser side of him was still a secret.

I ran the length of six houses to a park where I often went for refuge. Tears poured down my cheeks as I plopped myself onto the swing set in front of the tallest tree in the park and began to pump. I often went to this swing when I felt helpless. I'd pump out my anger harder and harder as though I were trying to reach the sky, with tears streaming out of my innocent child eyes. I knew there was nothing I could do. There was *never* anything I could do.

So I couldn't tell anyone about the joint, for fear of another frying pan incident. Or something worse.

Josh and I never spoke about the ride.

As a small child, I had developed a deep interest in softball. I'd begun playing city ball when I was seven and got very good at the sport. By the time I was twelve, coaches were beginning to notice me.

The summer before my thirteenth birthday, I was asked to join a traveling softball team playing shortstop. I ended up being the youngest player on the team and was only able to be a part of it because the coach went above and beyond to get me there. I was so excited when he showed up at my house one afternoon. I hid, listening to the conversation as he explained the team and the amount of travel to my mom.

But when I heard him say I'd need a parent with me on these trips, my heart sank. I knew the lifestyle my dad lived and the workload my mom took on would not line up with an activity like this.

When my mom confirmed my thoughts out loud, the coach, to my surprise, offered to be my guardian when traveling. My parents agreed to let me play, and I was ecstatic that I would have something to look forward to in life. I loved playing this game. It became my focus and was a way for me to escape my reality.

We traveled all over Ohio. Parents of other players on this team took care of me. The moms would braid my hair for the games and apply their child's sunblock to my fair, freckled skin. When I sank to the ground on those hot summer days from heat exhaustion and low blood sugar, grandpas would carry me off the field and grandmas would give me Gatorade and home-made chocolate chip cookies. Mothers put cold towels around my neck and nursed me until I was awake and ready to play.

My parents didn't know how much I needed them, but I never wanted to tell them because the love I was getting from others was far too comfortable to ruin. I experienced more joy on that traveling team than I had ever known before. The team and those parents became my family. I looked forward to being picked up and taken away for the weekend with other families but always dreaded the ride home.

My first year of high school, I made our varsity team, again playing shortstop. I was so excited that I had been recognized for my talent and hard work. Unfortunately, I had also begun partying by this time and had adopted the same habits as my dad and brother.

The weekend before conditioning started, I got so drunk at a party that when my best friend's dad picked us up to take us home, I threw up in his car. It was obvious that I was wasted. We lived in a very small town, and word traveled fast. That happened on a Friday night, and by Monday morning, I was kicked off the high school team.

I was completely devastated, but I couldn't let anyone know. I had developed this tough-girl facade by then and laughed it off, acting proud of how much Mad Dog 20/20 I had consumed and survived that weekend.

Truth be told, I had never felt so ashamed as when I saw my traveling team coaches for the first time after that incident. They had believed in me and invested their time and love in me. I had let them down. The coaches never said anything to me about it, but they didn't have to. I knew them well enough, and I could see the disappointment on their faces. This broke my heart and made me feel like such a loser.

After being kicked off the team, there was nothing holding me back. I drank and smoked in excess. I didn't care how much I would vomit or how horrible I felt the next day. Just being able to escape life for a little while was worth it to me.

As I got older and continued hanging out with the crowd I fit in with, my innocence disappeared. The habits I'd been forming to cope with the mess I was living were becoming a problem, and I became known around town as a bad influence within my peer group.

By the time I was sixteen, the physical abuse in my house had gotten unbearable, and the verbal abuse was pure torture.

My sophomore year, I was asked to a school dance. I felt so excited as I slipped into the beautiful bright-blue silk dress that sparkled from top to bottom, and then into my high heels. I stood in my bedroom listening to the song "Cowboy Take Me Away," by the Dixie Chicks, twirling and smiling in front of my mirror that leaned against the wall. I sang the words to the song softly, imagining the night I was about to experience.

When all my curls seemed just right and I felt happy with my appearance, I bounced down the stairs and into the living room. I came face-to-face with my dad, who was getting up from his designated seat on the couch.

I forced a crooked smile and eagerly waited for the compliments that anyone would expect, feeling as beautiful as I did.

But instead, he rolled his eyes and chuckled, turning his head away from me. Under his breath, he angrily muttered, "You look like a whore."

I was crushed. I stared at the floor with tears welling in my eyes. I didn't understand.

As I stood there, wordless and hurt, the doorbell rang. My date stood on the front steps waiting for me to appear. I walked to the door and opened it, wiping the tears away and trying to smile again.

I went to the dance that night and did my best to act like I was just as happy to be there as everyone else. But deep down, I couldn't wait to get out of there and attend the after-party, where I could drown my emotions in alcohol.

By the time I was seventeen, the abuse had finally taken its toll on my mom, and she let me know we would be moving out of my childhood home. She served my dad dinner on the couch, and then we left. I'm not sure why, but Josh stayed.

At this point, Josh and I didn't talk much and would only see each other from time to time at parties thrown by mutual acquaintances. When I did run into him, it felt like I didn't even know him. He and I were both so intoxicated during these encounters that we equally hid our pain, even from each other.

Mom and I packed a few things to get by and moved in with her mom—my grandmother, whom we had always called Mamaw. I didn't know Mamaw very well, but I welcomed the move anyway, knowing that I would be with my mom and away from our abuser. The adventure of moving out of the only bedroom I had ever known and the only house I had ever lived in was thrilling, as I was leaving nothing good behind.

Mamaw lived in a different town about twenty minutes down the road. She had a big home, which she occupied by herself.

Mamaw was originally from Harlan, Kentucky, and was as straight a shooter as you will ever meet. She was a very pretty lady, tall and slender with shiny black hair that was always worn in a pixie cut before pixies were cool. Her deep southern accent was sometimes hard to understand but always enjoyable to listen to.

It was interesting living with Mamaw. It felt as though we were starting over and that our lives could be different, that maybe we could even be happy.

I began spending time with Mamaw and my mom at the kitchen table, listening to them talk about the situation. Mamaw chain-smoked Menthol 100s, and I joined her with my own pack of Marlboro Lights. They talked about my dad. I puffed and listened. They revealed things about the situation that I had never known. These conversations only increased my hatred toward my dad and my desire to forget his existence.

Unfortunately, we didn't stay long. After one apologetic phone call from my dad promising change, Mom decided to move us back to our old house. This was hard. I didn't want to go back, but I had no choice.

Before sunrise the first morning back in our home, I woke to loud yelling. I took off my headphones and listened intently for my cue to run and help. I had learned by then that if it was only yelling and slamming doors, I wasn't needed. But when the thuds came and the house shook, I would feel a sense of urgency.

The worst feeling I ever had as a child was the helplessness of watching my mother—my favorite person on earth, my heart—get shoved to the ground. I would rather have taken a fist to my face than witness that. So when the thud came that morning, I ran down the stairs.

I found them right outside the kitchen doorway. My mom picked herself up off the floor and looked at me with ashamed, tear-filled eyes.

I screamed at them with tears flowing down my cheeks. "Is this the change? Is this why we came back? This will never change! I hate this. I hate this house. I hate this family!"

I ran back up to my room and sobbed with my face in my pillow. How was I ever going to get away from this life?

Luckily, only a couple of months later, in my senior year of high school, Mom realized that my dad hadn't changed and didn't intend to. His promises of change were only made to regain the control he desired over our lives. Mom talked to Mamaw again about moving back in with her, but this time Mamaw came up with a plan. She encouraged my mom to find an apartment down the road from her house. Mamaw would explain years later that it wasn't that she didn't want us there, but she thought if Mom had to sign a lease and pay for an apartment, it would be harder for her to keep going back and forth.

Mamaw was right. We never moved back.

Chapter Two

Smoke and Clouds

Moving day was awkward. A close friend of mine came to help move the rest of my things out of my bedroom. We were just a couple of high school kids and not very strong. As we struggled to get furniture down the stairs and out the front door, my dad sat on the couch snickering. Watching us with squinty eyes as he enjoyed his buzz and the show that we were giving him with our struggles, he never offered to help with the heavy loads. This infuriated me.

When we arrived at the new apartment, I felt as if a heavy weight had been lifted from my soul. The apartment was fresh, clean, brightly lit, and our opportunity for a new start. I imagined the fun my mom and I would have and the new memories we could make together.

Josh still stayed at the house. He was nineteen by then and

settling into a life of addiction himself, leaving him comfortable there. I just knew that this was it. Mom and I were free, and free to be happy and live the peaceful life I so desired.

But only a short time after we moved into the apartment, Mom informed me that she was seeing a man. I remember feeling both excited and apprehensive at the news. I wanted her to be happy, and she deserved to be treated better. But I couldn't help wondering what this meant for me. I feared losing her.

The man she was dating lived about an hour away from our apartment, and soon she began to go see him after work instead of coming home. I encouraged her, thinking this would be a good change for our lives. I had my own life with my friends taking up a lot of my time anyway. But at seventeen, I didn't know what was best. I started coming home from school to an empty one-bedroom apartment, where I would be by myself for days at a time. I wasn't paying the bills, but it still seemed like my apartment.

At first, I thought this was great. I'd pack the place with friends and boys, and we'd party until the wee hours of the morning, then show up to school hungover. But the apartment got old, and when the other parents caught on to what was happening, my friends were not allowed over anymore.

The move that I had welcomed became a huge inconvenience. The apartment was twenty minutes from my hometown, where I was still attending high school.

When I got tired of being alone, I'd pack my car with my belongings and move around from one friend's house to another. I stayed the night with whoever would let me and eventually just stored my clothes in the back seat of my car. I chose homelessness above loneliness.

I made sure to stay busy and to have other people around, avoiding the fact that my family was broken, and my understanding of life was worse than ever. The more time I spent away from family, the more I sought attention from anyone who would give it to me.

I eventually found myself hanging out at the home of a man who was a stranger but lived in my hometown. My bad habits had been leading me to places I shouldn't have been, especially at my age. I still have no idea how old this man was, but he had facial hair, a full-time job, and a house. The table in his home where I sat to do homework on the weekdays was used for playing cards, drinking, and doing drugs on the weekends.

Once I started coming around this man, he began giving me attention. He would comment to his friends about my looks, loud enough for me to hear. Getting attention, even in small doses, from this older man was oddly fulfilling. I had craved attention and had been rejected for so long that when this positive attention came, it struck my heart.

He started offering for me to stay the night, and before I knew it, I was living with him. We stayed high and drunk anytime we were together. It felt good to be with someone instead of sleeping in that apartment alone.

At bedtime each school night, this older man would pick up my limp, stoned body off the floor, fling me over his shoulder, and tuck me into bed. He would wrap his arms around me and comfort me through the night, never asking for anything in return.

In the morning, he'd wake me up in time to get ready for school before he headed to work. The thing I remember most about him is that he would wake me every morning with a hug that seemed to last forever. I so needed that hug each day, and the length of them seemed to make up for a lifetime of missing affection.

He was kind to me and took care of me, but I was in no condition to form a relationship.

After living with the man for a couple of months, I lay in bed one morning until I heard his truck pull away. I sat up and stared down the hallway, trying to find clarity about what was happening. I glanced at the bedside table and noticed that he had left me a freshly rolled joint to smoke before school.

Normally, that would have excited me, but for some reason that day, something inside me shivered, and I felt fear creep into my sober state for the first time since my life had completely fallen to pieces.

In a haze, which had become my natural state, I walked to the bathroom to shower before school. While in the shower that morning, I felt everything that had happened in the past couple of months start to finally sink in. I began to cry, struggling to make sense of what I was doing and what I was supposed to be doing. When reality set in that I was living with a man I didn't really know, fear took over. I had no idea where my mom was or if my dad knew I was living with a man. I hadn't talked to or seen my brother in months, and I could hardly remember the night before.

By the time I pulled into the parking lot at school—late, after a long, hot shower—all the other students were already in the building, settling in for a day of learning. Then I saw my mom glaring at me as she got out of her car.

As she made her way toward me, I noticed she looked awful. She had lost weight, and her face looked sunken in. But the way she carried herself was different. Her once sad, scared, weak disposition had turned hard and stern. She had obviously been waiting for me to show up. She didn't know where I had been living—I had kept up with her by phone but hadn't told her where I was. I could tell she was worried and mad and relieved to see me all at the same time.

Deep down, I felt relieved to see her as well, but I was a teenager and stubborn, and I wasn't going to shake the facade I clung to. She told me in her new stern tone that I needed to get back to the apartment where I was safe. I shot back with my rebellious attitude that there was no way I was going to be there alone anymore.

I turned away from her and walked into school, wiping secret tears. My homework was done. My body was clean. I appeared to have come from my home like all the other students, but my heart was breaking, and my soul was more lost than ever.

She was right; I shouldn't have been living with this man—who was now acting like we were married—but I didn't know where I belonged or what to do. He fulfilled something in my life that neither of us understood. Looking back, I know I only saw him as a getaway, someone who could supply my constant need to drown reality.

A couple of weeks passed after the conversation with my mom before I finally gave in. I went to the man's house after school one day toward the end of my senior year, grabbed a trash bag from his cupboard, and filled it with my belongings that had made it in from my car. I gathered my clothes out of his dresser and my toiletries out of his shower. Then it dawned on me that I had even bought dishes for "our" house. I took them too.

I had to get out. I ran to my car with the trash bag slung over my shoulder, like some drugged hobo. Standing by my car door, looking back at the house, I realized that was *exactly* what I had become.

As I backed out of his driveway, I saw his truck approaching. Fear instantly filled my body. I floored the gas pedal and drove off, kicking up gravel as I went. I didn't know what he expected of me or what his intentions were. I had never been around him sober, and the truth was, I wasn't being fair to him. He didn't know what my childhood had been like or even that I was running from my past.

He didn't come after me. My mom told me later that he had called when I left his house to let her know I was coming home. Apparently, he had snuck on my cell phone to get her number. I didn't know it then, but I was being protected in ways I can never fathom.

As I pulled into the apartment parking lot, the man my mom was now dating, and who was another stranger to me, greeted me at my car. Mom had told me his name was Mark. He offered to help carry my things. I handed him the trash bag, feeling ashamed, and watched as he walked ahead of me into the apartment.

He was short, slender, nicely dressed, and older than my mom by a decade—already sporting a head of gray hair. He worked at the same hospital Mom did and was much different from my dad. He appeared quiet and pleasant and seemed to really want to help me, but I didn't know how to process any of this new life. I didn't want to be there, but I was relieved not to be in the house I had just come from. I didn't want to be with my grandmother, who was another stranger at the time, and I didn't want to be back in the house with my dad and brother.

As I walked behind the new man-stranger carrying my belongings to the apartment door, I looked down and noticed I was scrawnier now at eighteen than I had ever been before. My pants barely hung on to my hips as I walked into the apartment kitchen, and when I thought about it, I couldn't remember when I had last eaten. I was a mess, and my mom's face confirmed that when we made eye contact.

I grabbed my bag out of Mark's hands with attitude, shared a quick glance with my mom, and went upstairs. I didn't feel comfortable with them. Even though my mom was right there, she was not the mom I was familiar with anymore. I knew this was better for her—*he* was better for her—but I didn't know how to handle all that was going on in my life. I didn't know where I belonged. I had settled into playing the victim and was drowning in self-pity. I saw myself as a child being forced to deal with adult problems.

I was lost and felt more alone than ever.

I had removed myself from the house where I'd been staying, but the partying and the longing for the high that would mask my feelings were far from gone.

Months later, I graduated from high school. Oddly, I was awarded the honor of being voted "class clown" that year. Funny how that award seems to always go to the lost soul seeking any kind of attention. I had become the good-time girl, the funny girl at parties who would always push the limits. My insane urge to disappear from reality always manifested itself in overconsumption of alcohol and marijuana and resulted in me acting like an idiot. Which is the definition of funny to most high-school-age kids.

I had made the breaking of my world appear funny to others.

Mom and Mark came to my graduation, along with Mamaw and Josh. A couple of people mentioned that my dad was there, but he never came in. Instead, he watched from the sidelines of the football field where the ceremony was held.

Sometimes, I like to imagine him standing there, proud and smiling, as my humanities teacher led the commencement speech. When my name was called to receive my diploma, the teacher spoke about the chocolate pudding wrestling I had done as my senior project in his class.

I had plastered the floor with large pieces of pink construction paper and brought bags upon bags of pudding to make pudding angels and wrestle in with classmates. This made one of the biggest messes in classroom history. Secretly, I had chosen this as my project because we were supposed to share a talent, and I felt I had none, so I resorted to humor.

Thankfully, the teacher extended grace and granted me a passing grade. I thought for sure that was something my dad would have gotten a kick out of in his sober state, and I can't help but imagine him cupping his head in his hands, laughing at this story. But I will never know if he was there.

So I graduated, but I had no plans for my future. I began working full time at a nursing home kitchen, delivering meals. My dad's mother was a patient there in the Alzheimer's unit. I would pass her in the halls, acknowledging that I knew her, but with nothing more than a quick smile or hello.

She too felt like a stranger. I had only ever seen her on holidays and the few random times throughout my childhood when she and my grandfather showed up at our house to visit. They never made it inside—Dad always ordered us to get down and keep quiet, as if they were our enemies, until they gave up and drove away. He always made sure we kept the windows and curtains closed too, so even when these random visits occurred, they couldn't see in. I later learned this was to avoid anyone smelling or seeing the drugs.

In spite of the Alzheimer's, my grandmother remembered that my mom had left my dad. I knew this because sometimes when I entered the unit, she would start hollering and crying. "I can't believe your mom would do this. I can't believe what she's doing to my son."

To my knowledge, she didn't know why we had left or how he had treated us. I never would have told her, but I think if

I did, she wouldn't have remembered or maybe even believed it. Dad was different outside the home. Around other people, he acted like a person I would have liked. No one knew our family secrets, and by that time, the story in town was that my mom had left him to be with another man.

Anyway, my grandmother's outbursts put me in an uncomfortable situation. But I needed the job to keep money in my pocket for booze and other habits, and gas in my car to get me out of that hateful town I was living in.

As time went on, other members of the family would come in to visit my grandmother. They would just give me a quick wave, acknowledging that they knew me, then turn to avoid any more awkwardness. This didn't bother me too much, since other than recognizing their faces, I really didn't know them either.

Until one day when I punched in the numbers to enter the Alzheimer's unit. The door opened, and I noticed my dad and his whole side of the family standing around my grandmother singing "Happy Birthday."

I imagine I probably looked like I had seen a ghost. I hadn't spoken to him or even seen him since my mom and I had left that last time, and I suddenly felt like the frightened child again.

As they all turned to see who had come in, I prepared myself for a fake smile and maybe even a wave. But no one said anything to me or even really acknowledged I was there. They just went on with the festivities, as if I were only a kitchen worker. Not one of them spoke to me. I didn't let it show, but this left me wounded and hurt, maybe more than I had ever been. My dad, who had trained us to hide from this family, now stood beside them, acting the part.

I walked out of that unit still feeling like a child, only now wearing scrubs and a hairnet, playing the role of adult, again with tear-filled eyes and a troubled heart.

All I could think was, what had I done?

Not long after I graduated, Mom and Mark decided they needed space of their own to start fresh, as they were planning a wedding. I dragged my feet on packing my things. I didn't want to go; didn't want another change. I couldn't help but feel betrayed when I arrived home from work one day to find the apartment empty. I called my mom to find out what was going on.

Apparently, everyone had decided—everyone but me—that I would move back in with Mamaw. Mom and her now fiancé would move down the road into a trailer. Although small, the trailer had an extra bedroom that could have been mine.

I was furious as she explained that my brother had graciously agreed to come help move my things. I felt I was being shuffled around, out of everyone's way. I was only eighteen, I had no direction in my life, and I again felt unwanted and unloved.

I couldn't afford my own place yet and didn't want to put myself in another bad situation, so I just obeyed. My clothes, my books, my journals—all of it had been gone through, boxed up, and dropped off. There I was, living with Mamaw again, only this time, it was just her and me.

I cried as I walked up the stairs to my new bedroom, still in shock at what had happened while I was at work.

From below, Mamaw said with a stern but sincere voice, "It's not like you're in jail."

I didn't even look at her as I continued up the stairs. It didn't feel like any of this was real, but I didn't feel like I was in jail either. I felt like an unwanted dog.

I walked into a room full of boxes and an unmade bed, disgusted at the mess of things waiting for me. I dropped to the floor, sobbing, then began digging through the mess to find clothes so I could get out of my filthy scrubs. Another piece of my heart had shattered.

Anger grew inside me, building into a grudge that I would hold on to for years to come.

These events helped me to rationalize the masking of my emotions by drowning my sorrows and confusion in poison. I continued working, partying, and driving back and forth between towns. When drug tests rolled around at work, I would chug gallons of water and cranberry juice to rid my system of any evidence. I didn't see my dad and brother. I rarely saw my mom. And my friends and former classmates were beginning new adventures of their own. I was alone.

Except for Mamaw. As I got comfortable with my new living situation, I began to stay for longer and longer periods at her house. She introduced me to coffee, and we spent hours at her kitchen table, drinking coffee, smoking cigarettes, and getting to know one another.

I grew to love Mamaw more than I had ever anticipated. She became the first person in my life to feel like home.

Chapter Three

The Dreamer

In 2003, I moved into my own place. Mom and Mark, who was now my new stepdad, had decided to move into a bigger home, so they gave me the trailer they had been living in. This trailer was presented as some sort of gift to me, but I felt like this was just a way for them to remove the burden of my existence on Mamaw.

In their defense, I always played it off cool, like I would never have wanted to intrude in their new life together. But I was scared living by myself. Those first few weeks alone were anything but comfortable. At night, I would lie in my bed in the back room with covers up over my head, shaking in fear. Every unfamiliar noise elevated my heart rate. Every horrifying thought of what happens to young girls when they're alone held my mind and body captive.

Although I yearned to be with someone, I had been separated from everyone. I was considered an adult by the world's standards, but I hadn't dealt with any of the hurt from my childhood. I felt stuck in victim mode.

My mom had helped me move into the trailer and got me an application for enrollment in a community college down the road. She also made some phone calls to help me get a better job working in the kitchen at a big hospital so I could afford to live on my own. I went along with whatever she threw my way because I couldn't think straight. All I focused on was the next party, where I could be with other people and drink until I was numb enough that I didn't care again.

At nineteen, I began paying my own bills, mowing my own grass, cleaning my own home, and buying my own groceries, which consisted of fruit snacks, Hot Pockets, and Vanilla Coke.

I attended nursing classes at the community college in the mornings and worked a forty-hour-a-week job in the evenings. I didn't want any of this, but not knowing what I *did* want, I just did as I was told. I knew Mom was trying to point me in the right direction, but I was hung up on why I had to be away from everyone. All I knew was that I still really wanted to be wanted. Growing to accept the lie that I was unwanted and unworthy of love, I pulled as far away from my family as I could and consumed as many substances as it took to lessen my fear of being alone.

When I got off work after my second-shift job at the hospital, I would run back to my hometown to meet with friends and party with every bit of energy I had left. I eventually found myself hanging out most of the time at a house with another older man. He went by the name of Boone.

Boone was the most easygoing person I had ever met, and

his calm demeanor made me comfortable. Sometimes it would be him and me there; other times the house would be full. Everyone in town knew it was the place to go, as Boone was a friend to everyone, and the party was always happening.

He had two younger brothers, who were often there. Brandon was the youngest, and Jayson was the middle brother. Jayson moved into the upstairs apartment of Boone's house shortly after I started coming around.

It took me a long time to figure Jayson out. He was different from anyone I had ever met before. He had long blond hair and big muscular arms, and played guitar. He was driven and focused, and the first person I had ever met who had dreams and talked about how he would reach them. At first, he came off as cocky, but the more I got to know him, the more I realized I was mistaking confidence for cockiness. I had never met anyone with such an enormous amount of confidence.

Jayson worked for a country radio station as a disc jockey, which was impressive, as he was only a year older than me. I would turn on the radio at work and brag to my coworkers that the man on the radio was a friend of mine. He loved his job, but his dream was to become a famous musician, as his passion was playing the guitar. He would party with us and was wild himself, but he also had a sense of maturity and focus that drew me to him.

The more I got to know Jayson, the more I realized he was determined to fulfill his dreams no matter what it took. He played in bands and went to concerts. He was always pushing everyone to get out of the house and not be lazy. We were all very content doing what we were doing, but he could make us question ourselves as we sat around Boone's house, high and numb.

Jayson had a desire to live. He talked about dreams and opportunities as though they were things within reach. That intrigued me because I came from a family who did nothing. We never had family adventures or went on any real vacations. And we certainly never talked about things like dreams or life ambitions.

This new bright optimism that Jay introduced me to left me hungry for more.

As 2003 wrapped up, I turned twenty years old, still working at the hospital, living in the trailer, and partying more than ever. My neighbors at the trailer park had caught on to me and started showing up at my door sometimes just to make sure I was alive. There were mornings I woke up to them pounding on my door. I'd be lying on the kitchen floor, not sure how I got there. Still dizzy from the poison I had dumped into my body the night before, I'd crawl to the door to answer, afraid that if I didn't, the cops would be knocking it down to check my pulse. Satisfied that I was still alive, the neighbors would leave, and I'd be alone again. I remember looking in the mirror one of those days and realizing I didn't recognize the person staring back at me.

Although the voice that had always been with me as a child had disappeared when we left my childhood home, I could still find the presence of *something more* in my eyes. And even though my growing-up years had left me feeling like a victim, I was now making my own bad choices that only made matters worse.

But there came a day when I began to feel change from the life I had always known.

It was a Saturday, and like most other weekend afternoons, my friends and I were at Boone's house. The sun warmed the living room through the window. Strumming the song "Pictures," by Kid Rock and Sheryl Crow, Jayson announced that he had landed a gig and he needed a band fast.

When he got to Sheryl's part in the song, he said, "Here's the problem. I really want to play this song, but I need a girl to sing."

I remember, like it was yesterday, saying, "I can sing!"

I had always known I could sing. I loved to sing, and it was just something that came naturally to me. I knew the song very well, as it had been overplayed on the radio at the time. When Jayson got to the "girl" part in the song, I sang loudly and confidently. He decided I was good enough for the part, and just like that, I was in a rock band!

Before long, Jayson had formed a full band, and with all the practicing we had to do, I ended up spending a lot more time with him.

The first time we were onstage and sang that song in public, sparks flew. There was chemistry between Jayson and me, and we realized that, with his guitar skills and my singing, we had something people were interested in. Maybe we were meant for each other.

One afternoon, as we finished band practice, I asked Jayson to teach me how to play guitar. I figured, if I could play, maybe I could accompany myself singing. He was on board and suggested we hop in the band van, go camping for an evening, and work on this skill. I was up for anything at this time, so as any responsible person would do to prepare for a day away at camp, we grabbed a gallon jug of fruit punch and a bag of chips and hit the road.

We drove down dark country roads and eventually pulled into a campground. We didn't venture out but stayed up half the night talking and plucking a little on the guitar in the van. When we were too tired to keep our eyes open, we curled up in the back. Jayson gently wrapped his muscular arm around my body, holding tight enough to make me feel warm and safe. I knew then that there was something different about him than anyone else I had dated.

I didn't know what it was, but it made me feel safe and happy.

The next morning, we opened our eyes to warm daylight—and a large group of people peeking in the van windows. When we figured out that these were Boy Scouts, we frantically slumped down, trying to get away from their eyes, but it was no use. Apparently, we had parked right in the middle of a Boy Scout camp, and while it had been extremely quiet when we pulled in, it was now stirring with lots of little boys in uniform.

We lay there for a moment, staring blankly at one another, then laughed until our stomachs hurt. When Jayson got himself together, he hopped into the driver's seat and sped off out of the campsite. I stayed where I was, laughing.

When we were safe and out of sight of the Boy Scouts, I hopped up into the passenger seat, still giggling in disbelief at what had just happened. We were in the same clothes from the day before, with no water or toothbrushes, and just a little of our juice and chips left for "nourishment."

Stopping at a gas station, we attempted to get ourselves together as much as we could. Then Jayson suggested we go hiking in the state park we were driving through. Of course, I was up for anything, and I trusted him. We parked the van and started off on a trail with no supplies.

Early into our hike, Jayson suggested we get off the trail and do some exploring of our own. I didn't think twice about it. I had no idea what hiking even consisted of, and I trusted that he did.

A little more than an hour into our walk, I noticed he was acting panicked. I was so in awe of what I was seeing in those woods, I was almost too fascinated to care, but then I realized he was lost. He soon admitted that he had no idea how to get back to the trail but that he could figure it out. He then told me, for the first time that day, that he had to be to work that afternoon at the radio station, and we needed to hurry to get back to the van.

As I remember this moment, I'm pretty sure we didn't talk; we just ran. But in my mind, there was loud, intense music playing over those woods. We jumped over tree stumps, slid in the mud, changed direction once, then twice, then three times.

When we came upon a slippery, mossy cliff—that I thought was way too high to jump from—without hesitation, Jayson jumped and rolled.

Once he was up and had gathered himself, he yelled, "Come on!"

There was no way I was going to jump off that cliff, but before I could say no, my two-dollar Old Navy flip-flops betrayed me, and I went down on my bottom and slid fast. Jay still remembers this moment, saying that I laughed the whole way down, with my hands up in the air like I was on a roller coaster.

I couldn't stop myself. I slipped and slid and eventually glided right off the cliff to where Jay waited with open arms. He caught me, but we both went down, and I landed right on top of him, squashing his body with mine. This I do remember clearly—I was still in one piece. I'd knocked the wind right out of him, but I didn't even have a scratch. He didn't think it was very funny, but I laughed until I cried while he lay there, trying to catch his breath.

We were lost in those woods, but Jayson was still gaining my trust more and more. Hours passed in that forest before we finally heard cars and found the road.

Jayson and I were becoming best friends, as our feelings for one another grew.

One morning, about a week after this camping trip, I woke up in my trailer and made my way to the kitchen to start some coffee—Mamaw had gotten me hooked. The curtains were gently blowing at the open window, and the aromatic smell of fresh-cut grass was wafting through the screen.

As I entered the kitchen, I noticed a plate covered with foil on my tiny table. On top was a paper folded in half. I took the foil off, revealing a wonderful-looking breakfast that was still warm. The note on top was from Jayson, explaining that he had just had breakfast at his grandma's house and thought of me. He had come to my trailer that morning to slip breakfast through my window.

My heart swelled. No one had ever gone out of their way for me like that. I couldn't help but smile. I poured a cup of hot coffee and ate my breakfast by myself, but I didn't feel lonely at all anymore.

Our friendship grew into a relationship, and we continued to play in the rock band together. We were both working full-time jobs, and I was still taking college classes. We had a lot of fun together, but there came a point—which to me appeared out of nowhere—when Jayson said that we should probably stop smoking pot. My crazy, carefree attitude was starting to worry him, he said, and I was a confusing person when I was high. I was not thrilled about this idea, but I didn't want to lose him, so I agreed to slow down.

As we eased into this new way of living, we realized that it would require us to back away from the group we were used to. We found ourselves alone but together. As we wandered away from the old crowd, it only made sense that Jayson would move in with me, since he was at my trailer more than he was at his own apartment, which was where temptation lived.

We began to embrace this partnership and ventured out of our norm, taking trips out of state and exploring other avenues to keep ourselves busy. The thrill of packing up our car on a Friday afternoon and driving all night from Ohio to Nashville, Tennessee, became a common routine for us.

I loved spending time with Jayson, and I was caught up in all the adventures that came with it. He and I were calming down and growing into adulthood together, while growing to love one another.

One evening in 2004, as we returned to the trailer from dinner, Jay reached into his pocket and rested his hand there for a long time. I asked him what he was hiding.

"Nothing." He grinned playfully.

I knew he was hiding something, so I pushed him to tell me. When I realized he wasn't giving in, I lunged at him to try to wiggle my hand into his pocket, which resulted in a wrestling match in the doorway.

Finally, after we were worn out from the rumble, he gave in and let me reach into his pocket without a fight. I pulled out a diamond ring.

I instantly regretted my persistence. I mean, I obviously thought I loved him and loved being with him, but after witnessing the mess with my own parents, marriage wasn't something I saw as a good thing. And we were young. We had no plans and no direction in life. We were just wild and free.

But when he asked me with a shy smile to marry him, I said yes.

We slowly started to plan a wedding, including purchasing a house that we really couldn't afford. This was my idea. I thought if we were going to get married and start a new chapter in our life, we should have a new place to live. That meant getting out of that trailer park where I had never wanted to be in the first place.

Lucky for us, banks were loaning to people who really shouldn't have been able to get a loan. We couldn't afford the house we asked for, even though it was a repo, but they gave it to us anyway.

Jayson fixed what needed to be repaired, and I cleaned the flea-infested house.

We did what we could and moved in our furniture, which was only enough to fill one bedroom and half a living room. We were happy with the house and felt blessed to be able to get it, but it overextended us financially. The reality of being adults was sinking in fast, and the stress settled in. We began fighting, and my doubts about marriage grew. But we pressed on, feeling too far into the relationship to quit.

We decided the wedding would be in the backyard of Jayson's childhood home, right in the middle of the woods where he had spent so much time as a kid.

We were young and in love, but also immature and inexperienced. Jayson had dreams, and they all consisted of playing music. I carried baggage that often came out in my emotions, the intensity of which only grew as I quit the drugs that helped me forget. We had not discussed children or our future, or our pasts. We had no idea of the very hard lessons we would have to go through to understand the meaning of life. We knew nothing about the journey we were about to begin.

Chapter Four

The Last Words

"When you're alone on your deathbed, you're going to wish you hadn't treated me this way."

These haunting words that so easily flew off my tongue on the day I went to reconcile with my dad wound up being the last thing I would ever say to him.

I had made a point sometime after the divorce to make amends with my dad. But when my plans didn't go as I had anticipated, I vowed in anger that would be the last time I ever saw him.

To my surprise, my feelings changed on June 4, 2004, when I heard that my dad's mother had passed away. I felt that I needed to attend the funeral.

As I prepared my mind and heart to see this side of the family again, I remembered the last conversation between my dad and me. I had finally conjured up enough bravery to return to my childhood home. Even though I despised that house, as my dad had crushed the souls of all who lived within those walls, I had started to feel an urgency to patch things up with him.

I thought enough time had gone by that we could talk about mistakes that had been made and try to begin healing some wounds. As I parked in front of the house, I questioned the idea. The fear associated with this place churned in my gut.

After a few moments of wrestling with whether to get out of the car, I decided I wasn't a child anymore and I needed to try. I had been changing and maturing. I felt confident that I could lead the conversation and keep it positive.

I got out of the car and walked up to the door with my head held high. I knew it would be weird if I knocked, so I let myself in.

Only a few steps inside, I made eye contact with my dad. I could tell I had surprised him, as he seemed uneasy. I asked if we could talk, with my head still high, and forced the shakiness to leave my body. He agreed.

We settled in at the kitchen table. I looked around, noticing that nothing had been changed since we moved out. Sitting there reminded me of all the times my family had fought while trying to eat a meal together.

I'd dreaded going to that table on birthdays. They would always begin with singing and end with screaming. We were not allowed to laugh at the table. When my brother and I were young, we would giggle at each other through the bottoms of our drinking glasses as our milk slid to one side. The laughing wouldn't last long before we would get slapped, yelled at, and then—if we were lucky—sent away.

On this day, as my dad and I sat there, it became obvious that he was high. He always had an evil look in his eyes when he was high, and I had to squelch the childlike fear that bubbled in my body, wondering when he would snap. But I reminded myself that I was braver and bigger, and most of all, I had a getaway car right outside the door if I needed it.

We began to talk.

I started by saying, "I came here to try to fix our relationship, Dad."

He just looked at me.

I continued. "I'm older now, and we both know all the crap that went on in this house."

He still just stared.

As I began to cry, I swallowed hard, struggling for what more I needed to say. I looked into his eyes and lost my breath when I realized there were tears there as well. He reached over and put his hand on mine, leaving me completely still. I didn't recognize this touch.

We sat there for a moment in an awkward silence.

I scrambled for something else to say, but he looked at me and began to mouth words. I felt my heart preparing for the apology I had been waiting on my whole life.

But instead, his familiar sarcastic grin appeared, and he asked, "How's your new daddy?"

I was done.

I stood up, no longer able to hold my head high, and explained that I didn't even live with them. I was on my own and moving on. Angrily, I reminded him that I had come there to try to work things out. He didn't know what I had gone through since the divorce. He didn't know how lonely I had been or that I had run to the same poison that had consumed his whole life to try to deal with my emotions. He didn't realize he had wounded me deeply and that all I desired from him was love.

He would never give in; he didn't have it in him. He chose to stay angry. I was angry too, but looking back, I wish I would have just left him like that; with the burden of the last words of hurt on his shoulders.

But I didn't.

Instead, I lashed out furiously.

"When you're alone on your deathbed, you're going to wish you hadn't treated me this way."

I knew the moment that came out of my mouth that I would never talk to him again. My pride would never let me do it.

> Be careful what you say and protect your life. A careless talker destroys himself.
> Proverbs 13:3 GNT

What I *didn't* know was that I would relive that moment again and again for almost fifteen years. Those words would never leave my memory, and I would never forget that conversation.

As Jayson and I prepared to go to the funeral, I could tell he was just as nervous as I was. He had never met or even seen my dad, other than in pictures, and we both knew this would be uncomfortable.

We walked into the church I had known as a child, and I couldn't help but focus on the enormous picture depicting Jesus on the wall. My mom had cleaned this church as a side job when I was young, and I would always run from this picture in fear, feeling like the eyes were following me everywhere I went. I didn't feel any different walking in as an adult.

Jay and I made our way to a pew in the middle of the sanctuary. I didn't have much emotion, as my grandmother had been a stranger to me most of my life, but I noticed family members sitting in the front row facing the casket. Everyone I had last seen in that nursing home sat there together as they had been when they were singing to her.

My brother turned and smiled a crooked, sad smile at me, then faced forward again. I didn't even feel like I knew him anymore. I focused directly on the back of my dad's head and made sure to position myself as far away from him as I could. I didn't hear anything the preacher said. All I could focus on was my dad. Thoughts raced through my mind. Did he even know I was there? Would I be able to slip in and out without his noticing? What would I say if he spoke to me? *Would* he speak to me?

About halfway through the funeral, he turned around as though he knew I was looking at him and, without emotion, turned back to face the casket as if I weren't there. Bitterness grew in my soul as my heart turned to stone.

Jayson and I stayed for the entire service. When it was over and people started to leave, I remained seated, waiting to see if he would look my way again.

He didn't.

I didn't understand my yearning for him to acknowledge me. But when nothing came, I began to cry. Suddenly, I was overwhelmed by the emotions you should have at a funeral, but mine were not for the deceased, but for the living. I whispered to Jayson that I was ready to leave. He said nothing but got up and followed me out the door.

That was the last time I saw my dad alive.

October 5, 2005, started out as any normal day for Jayson and me. He was already at work by the time I woke up. The sun was out, but it was cool enough for a light jacket. The leaves had begun to change, and we were in my favorite season in Ohio: fall.

I felt good. My health was great. I was engaged to be married. Jay and I were getting comfortable in our new home, and everything in my life was okay, for once. I had managed to tuck my childhood memories, sadness, and unforgiveness somewhere that I couldn't find them.

I got ready for the day with upbeat music blasting through the house, then took off for my anatomy class at the community college. On my way there—with the sunroof open, singing loudly to the songs on the radio—I came to the intersection, where turning right would lead to my school, and turning left led to my hometown.

I had made this drive routinely for some time, and I hadn't been back to that house since the last conversation with my dad. But that morning, I paused. A voice inside told me, *Go see your dad.*

I shook it off. *No way.* Pride was strong. I wasn't speaking to him.

I made my decision, turned right, and went to class.

About a half hour into class, the door flew open, and everyone got quiet. A lady who worked in the school office stood there with a note in her hand.

In a loud, out-of-breath voice, she said, "I have an emergency message for a Ms. Heather Petersen."

My head shot up. Shocked that she was there for me, I gathered my things in anxious embarrassment.

She took me outside the classroom. "Honey, I have a note that you are to call your mom, at your dad's house."

I was puzzled. "Call my mom at my dad's house?" My mom and dad, to my knowledge, hadn't spoken since their divorce. My mind raced as I prepared to call my mom. All I could think was that something had happened to Josh.

As the phone rang, I began to panic. My body felt stiff, but my insides shook.

When Mom answered, I urgently forced out the words.

"Hey, what's going on?"

She was very calm. "I need you to get in your car and drive to your dad's house."

My insides shook more now than before. "Okay, but what happened?"

"I don't want to tell you yet." Her tone had sharpened. "I just need you to get here."

I didn't listen. "Is it Josh? Is he okay?"

"I'll talk to you when you get here," she insisted. "I don't want you stressed while you're driving."

"Well, it's a little late for that! Please, just tell me what's going on."

I heard a long sigh, then, "It's your dad, Heather." Her voice caught. "He's dead."

"What?" My entire body went limp, but my heart sped up.

Inside, I was relieved that it wasn't my brother, but to be honest, I couldn't believe that my dad was dead. This wasn't how my life was supposed to go. *I* was the victim, not him.

Angry notions swirled in my mind. He should have had to stay alive to feel the hurt that he had caused us our entire lives. He should have been the one experiencing the shock that *I* was dead and that he had been wrong for so long.

This wasn't fair. There was so much that had been left undone. He'd never apologized for ruining my childhood! He'd never shown any regret for the things he had done to me! He'd never admitted he was wrong or let on that he had any feelings of remorse. Why did *he* get to leave?

I was so angry, and that anger was torture.

I walked out of the school feeling like my insides were still on the floor where I'd stood when I heard the news. My limbs felt heavy and my head empty as I drove to the house.

Pulling up to my childhood home, I noticed there were

too many cars lining the road to park up front. I drove around back and parked in the driveway that extended from our backyard garage. There were other cars parked there as well that I didn't recognize, but one vehicle stood out. My dad's truck.

His truck was pulled all the way up to the back deck in the grass, leaving me to wonder why. I walked up the stairs, pushing my fear away, and entered through the back door. It was weird walking into the house. Nothing had changed. It still reeked of cigarette smoke and held our framed memories on the walls.

In the strangest way, the house felt more alive than it ever had. There were neighbors and family in the house. That had never been allowed. A breeze blew through the open doors and windows. The sun shone in because someone had broken his long-standing rule by opening the curtains.

I passed through the kitchen and saw our neighbor who had lived in the big white house next door my entire childhood, doing the dishes. She had been a cleaning lady for years. I'm sure when she walked into that house and noticed the filth from two men living there alone, her instinct said to clean. She looked at me for a moment, then went back to what she was doing.

I continued past the bathroom where I had almost ended my life, up the two stairs that I had always skipped in a hurry to get to a fight, and onto the landing, where I could always hear my dad snoring.

As I walked into my parents' old bedroom, I saw my mom, brother, grandpa, uncle, a preacher, a police officer, and a coroner. They were all silent and staring at the corpse of my dad, lying in his bed. My breath left me as my eyes caught the gray version of my dad.

He looked awful. His mouth was stuck open like he had died in the middle of a roar. His strawberry hair that had begun to whiten was a mess. He was dead, but I still saw a look of fear on his face, which instantly broke my heart and lessened my anger.

He was only forty-four when he died, twenty-four hours from his forty-fifth birthday.

I couldn't help but wrinkle my nose as I took in the stench that filled the air. The room stunk like urine mixed with another terrible smell I wasn't familiar with. The smell I would soon recognize as the smell of death.

Josh had woken up that morning and found our dad like that after realizing his truck was still there. Dad had been dead for hours.

They had called me to rush to the house because they thought I would want to see him before the coroner took him. I don't know if that was exactly what I wanted, but maybe that's common practice?

The preacher from my grandpa's church that we had attended those handful of times cleared his throat. "Let us pray before they take him."

Everyone in that room bowed their heads and closed their eyes like they knew what they were doing. I don't think they understood any more than I did. I couldn't move. I was scared. I kept thinking he was going to jump up and be so mad that everyone was in his room. I stayed close by the door so I could exit if need be. I felt stiff and couldn't close my eyes to pray. I couldn't take my eyes off him.

The preacher prayed. Again, I don't remember a word he said. We all took one last look at that terrible sight and left the room in single file, me leading the way.

A little while later, the coroner walked past us with my dad on a table with wheels, zipped up in what looked like a big black trash bag. I sat on the couch, making sure to avoid the spot that was worn with my dad's designated indent. I watched passively, just as Dad had done when I moved my things out, as the men struggled to get his large body out the door and down the stairs.

I asked my mom as they wheeled the body away why the truck was in the middle of the backyard. She explained sadly that Josh had told her that the night before, Dad had bought an oddly large amount of groceries. Josh said that when Dad returned home with them, he could barely walk the length from the truck to the backdoor, even though he had parked as close as he could get. After Dad had gotten them all in the house, he took a shower and went to bed.

Josh explained to us that the items Dad bought were not the regular things he would get at the grocery store and that he had never bought that much food in one trip. The cupboards were bursting.

It appeared that Dad was preparing for Josh to be alone.

Jayson made it to the house when they were bagging the body. I'd called him as soon as I got off the phone with my mom. He had only ever seen my dad at my grandma's funeral and had never been in this house. He had no idea the stories those walls could tell.

Just like that, my dad was gone. When they zipped that bag, they ended his story. Another story that God had written; a story I didn't know much about. There's so much I still don't know. Much of it, I would have changed for selfish reasons. But little by little, my dad's death began to unleash wonder and truth that I never saw coming.

The end of his life would be the beginning of my quest to find truth. It signaled the moment my spiritual journey began. Slowly, everything in my life started changing. I went from relief that the monster couldn't hurt anyone anymore to confusion like I had never known and lots of questions.

For the first time in my life, I began thinking of my dad as another person instead of some scary beast. Questions circled in my mind, over and over. How did he die? Why did this happen? Why didn't I try harder to make things right with him? Why didn't he try to make things right with me? Did he ever love me? Did he want to die? Was he scared?

He was alone.

He died alone, just as I had promised in my last words to him.

Chapter Five

Becoming His

Even though my mom had remarried by this time, she handled all the final arrangements.

When my brother and I walked into the funeral home with her for our planning appointment, a mortician handed me a brown paper bag containing my dad's clothes that he had been wearing when he took his last breath. I thanked the man for the gift he had given me and then carried it around for hours.

We picked out a casket and a tombstone, decided what pictures would be displayed and what music would be played during the service, determined calling hours, and discussed who would get up to speak.

After that, the three of us went to the house to go through my dad's belongings. There, I decided to open the bag that had been given to me. I stuck my nose down, trying to find the smell of grease and paper that my dad had always carried on him from his work. Instead, I found the smell of death. I gagged and rushed the bag to a trash can out at the curb. That disgusting scent would remain embedded in my sinuses.

While going through his belongings, Mom offered his cell phone to me. As I explored the calls and messages on his phone, I noticed that his number looked strangely familiar. Trying to recall where I had seen it, I looked on my own phone and realized my dad had called me not long before he passed!

Jayson and I were in our new home and had placed an ad in the paper to sell our trailer. I had missed a call one day and had called back in hopes that it was an inquiry about the trailer.

When the person answered, I said, "Hi, this is Heather Petersen. I had an ad in the paper about selling our mobile home. Were you calling about that?"

A male voice muttered, "No," followed by a long, awkward silence.

I apologized; then, uncomfortable with the silence, I said goodbye and hung up. I never knew until I put the pieces together with the number, that it was my dad I'd spoken to that day.

He had called me.

I had called him back, but I didn't even recognize his voice.

I couldn't help but mourn the idea that he had called to say he was sorry or to tell me he was sick and wanted to talk to me or even see me. I don't know what he was going to say, and I never will, but when I called him back and he realized I didn't even recognize his voice, I'm sure he gave up on me, as I had given up on him.

When the results from the autopsy arrived, I was astonished to learn that my dad had died of what is called *cardio-*

megaly. An enlarged heart. Ironically, my dad had died from the very thing I always thought he was lacking.

His days on earth were ended by a heart that was too big.

We saw him again a couple days later at his funeral, in the casket we had chosen. This sounds so morbid, but I couldn't wait to touch him.

At first glance, I noticed they had applied what appeared to be a pound of makeup to make his face appear alive again. They had put his glasses on him as if he would be needing them, and his mouth was closed. He had been cleaned up, not smelling of death anymore, and wore a sweater that we all thought he would never have picked out. It had been hanging in his closet with tags on it, making us wonder if he had a hunch this was going to happen.

I was the first one to get to the casket. I reached down and held his hand. I recognized the lines and the feel of his fingers from that day at the house when, for a moment, his touch had been gentle. This time though, it was cold and hard. I finally got the courage to lean down and hug him, only to find that under that ugly sweater was plastic where they had opened him up and gone through his insides for the autopsy. I didn't care. I gave that man a lifetime of hugs. I think if there were an award for the most hugs given to a corpse, I would have won.

He had never been in the right mind to give love; he never hugged or held hands. We'd all longed for that from him. I wasn't going to miss my opportunity for the very thing I had always desired from him. I was going to hug him as much as I could before they put him in the ground.

I walked around the funeral home that day, having an out-of-body experience. Tears constantly filtered out of my eyes as I watched the people coming to see my dead dad. Both familiar and unfamiliar faces poured into the funeral home. My group of close friends from school came together and filled a row. I could tell they didn't know what to say or do, and I didn't know what to say to them. None of us had ever lost a parent. This was uncharted territory.

The place was packed, and we later learned that over two hundred people had come to calling hours. All my life, I'd heard people say how much they liked my dad and how great a guy he was. Everyone outside of the family knew him as "Pete," giving him the nickname because his last name was Petersen; his legal first name was Gregory. Here, I saw proof of just how loved by others he had been.

The room was full of people who knew very well that I was not on good terms with my dad, but it was also a room full of tearful friends and family who had given up on him as well. These people had families of their own. They couldn't have given him the love and attention that he needed in full. I could feel their regret. I listened to them explain how they had tried to help him. But it was too late.

My dad had worked the same job in the same factory for eighteen years. The employees there knew him differently than we did at home; differently than his closest friends too. Those who were close to him explained that he had sunk deep into depression during those last years when we were not around.

My old neighbor, the cleaning lady, explained to me that Dad had confided in her that it hurt him that he hadn't received a Father's Day card in years. That confused me deeply.

Did he really expect that?

Or was it just a plea for sympathy from the neighbor?

A supervisor from his shop gave us a picture of my dad that had been taken about six months before his death. My heart broke even more when I saw him in that photo. He was severely overweight and hunched over like he had stared at nothing but the floor for years. He had a forced smile on his sad face and his arms crossed over his giant belly in what looked like an effort to hide some of what was there.

I hadn't seen or talked to him in years, but I knew him. This man had gone from intense anger to deep sadness. The expression on his face told a sad story. He had gotten older. His habits had caught up with him. His heart couldn't take any more abuse from his own hands. I could hardly bear the pain it caused me to look at the picture, but I couldn't resist the urge to keep searching his face for answers.

After speaking with multiple people, I realized I was hearing the same story over and over. His closest friends and family members had started to see what my mom, my brother, and I had seen our whole lives. A man who had lost himself and then lost his family, a man who was worn out from being so angry, a man who had battled addiction and had a story of his own.

I spoke at his funeral, but I didn't reminisce about all the good times or all the funny things he should be remembered for. Instead, at twenty-one years old, I quit crying long enough to be a stern speaker to a room full of breaking hearts. I preached from the podium to his friends that they could *not* have done any more. I preached to the room, explaining that we'd all tried, but he wouldn't accept our love. I didn't know where that strength came from then, but I somehow needed to give others peace, so they could go on and not live with regret. But I was taking the regret in full.

As I watched Jayson, the man I would soon marry, help escort my dad's casket to the hole where his body would be laid forever, I again felt time stand still. Regret burrowed deep into my heart as the shovels dumped dirt upon the man I didn't know how to forgive.

In the following weeks, my emotions were everywhere. I was deep into the mourning process. Pain settled in, and the questions started flowing all over again.

I wept tears that never seemed to end.

When I closed my eyes, I saw my dad's face. Not from life or from the casket. I could only see that terrible face from his deathbed. I imagined him calling me again, only this time I recognized his voice, and I wondered about all the possibilities that could have come from that conversation.

Then, my thoughts turned to horrified panic.

Where had he gone?

I still didn't know much, but I knew that in spite of his being dead and his body being in the ground, the real man who was my dad had gone somewhere else.

Jayson and I had been attending a church in our town for a couple of months before my dad's death. Merely a pew warmer, I still didn't understand what the preacher was talking about and, quite frankly, didn't care to pay much attention. I didn't own a Bible or have any desire to. But Jayson and I knew that we wanted a preacher to marry us, and for that to happen, we had to be attending a church.

After struggling with these thoughts long enough, I felt I needed to talk to the preacher. Mom called him for me one day when she noticed I was still struggling. She and I had begun to grow closer through the death of my dad, and she was becoming more concerned with how I was handling this tragedy. I think she was afraid I might sink into a deep depression, which I probably was. She asked the preacher and his wife to come to Sunday dinner.

This couple was still in their twenties, only a few years older than Jayson and me. After the meal, the preacher, his wife, and I went into another room to talk. I couldn't wait to ask him my most painful question, assuming he was like God himself and would have the answers.

As soon as we got settled, I blurted out, "Where did my dad go?" I sobbed like an out-of-control child.

The preacher and his wife looked at me like I was crazy. I felt like I was.

I said it again, a little louder this time. "Where did he go?"

The man looked at me and said, "Do you mean, heaven or hell?"

"Yes," I replied. "I'm scared he's in hell!"

As the words flew out of my mouth, my heart broke to pieces. This was my dad, and even though our relationship had been horrible, his blood flowed through me. I cared. I was realizing how much love I had for him, despite the hurt he had caused in his earthly body.

Painfully, it had taken his death for me to realize I not only loved him, but I believed in something greater than this life on earth.

The preacher asked, "Why would you think he's in hell?"

I explained that he was not a good man. I told them how he had treated us and explained that he drank and did drugs all his life.

While the preacher looked at me in disgust, his wife didn't say a word.

Finally, he answered. "Our God is a forgiving God. I don't believe your dad is in hell."

But I still doubted, realizing this preacher didn't know for sure either.

Weeks after we buried my dad, his brother came to visit me. I had never before had a visit from this man, who resembled my dad in so many ways. The conversation stayed focused on Dad's death, but my thoughts began to shift, and I began to feel some peace.

My uncle told me that the preacher of my grandpa's church, the one who was at the house when they took my dad away, had explained to him that my dad had gone to the church a couple of weeks before he died and asked to be baptized.

I couldn't believe it! I didn't understand baptism fully, but this gave me hope. Maybe his heart really had changed over those last couple of years. Maybe he had gotten so lonely and so desperate that he ran to the church to find God. This made my wondering grow, as I was beginning for the first time in my life to see my dad as a positive influence and God as a Savior.

After hearing this news, my heart was settled regarding his whereabouts. I didn't know where he was but felt settled that he was okay. He had probably gone to heaven. But the anger, hurt, and unforgiveness that I still had stored away in my heart was far from settled and tormented me every day.

It was in 2005 when I became so broken that I truly began to *wonder* about God and started my journey toward *becoming His*.

PART TWO

Looking Up

But you, God, see the trouble of the afflicted; you
consider their grief and take it in hand.
The victims commit themselves to you;
you are the helper of the fatherless.
Psalm 10:14 NIV

Chapter Six

Washed Up

By 2006, my mom and I were really working on mending our relationship. The more time we spent together, the more I realized she'd never had the chance to be herself when I was a child. The mom I had always known wasn't the person she desired to be. She had been broken as well. Mom was only eighteen when my brother was born and twenty when I came along. She'd been a baby herself, dealing with the same abuse we all experienced.

As we talked, I came to understand that she had done the best she could to help me in the time that I was sinking, trying to set me up for survival even as she navigated her own path. And she did the same for Josh after Dad's death.

Dad's house went up for sale, forcing Josh out of our childhood home and into a trailer of his own. This move, along with his share of the inheritance money, was a nightmare of open roads for Josh and his addiction.

I didn't see him much after my dad's death, but Mom did all she could to make sure his needs were met. She explained that she knew he was responsible for his own bad choices, but she couldn't stop being his mother. I understood that Josh was using the drugs to mask the feelings he didn't know how to deal with, just as I had. But again, there was nothing I could do. Watching my brother sink deeper into his addictions was one of the hardest and most frustrating things I've ever gone through.

The drugs got hold of Josh until he was no longer there. There was no doubt, these drugs were demonic. Trying to get involved or thinking I could solve his problems only hurt me and sent my own mental health spiraling back out of control. I had to step away from my relationship with him in order to keep my own sanity.

June 24, 2006, eight months after my dad's death, Jayson and I were married. My dad's brother walked me down the aisle in place of the dad who probably never would have. I still didn't know my uncle well, but allowing him to step in where my dad would have been expected felt right.

Jayson and I couldn't have dreamed up a more perfect day. We were married in the woods behind his parents' house, as we had planned. The rows of white chairs divided by an aisle of daisies—my favorite flower—were full of people we loved. The temperature was perfect, and the trees were beautiful shades of green. Our wedding pictures have an ethereal glow from where the sun shone perfectly through the branches that afternoon.

In November, I found out that I was expecting our first child. I knew my life needed to change. I could no longer participate in the habits I had formed. The partying would have to end. The late-night drinking and morning cigarettes with coffee would have to stop. I know I'm going to make this sound easier than it is for most people, and I don't discount the fact that addiction is a serious thing. I have witnessed it firsthand. But I just stopped. The day I found out I was expecting was the day I kicked the habits out of my life. At least for the time I would be carrying a child.

Which made me realize, *I was never addicted to the substances; I was addicted to what helped me forget.*

Jayson slowed down on this lifestyle also, as he welcomed the change that was coming in our lives. But when alcohol and partying were cut from our one-on-one time, our relationship changed.

As Jay and I spent time together sober, I felt as though we were being reintroduced to one another. We began taking walks out of boredom, and that encouraged deep conversation. This forced us to talk about life. These talks were revealing and personal. Prior to this, we'd seldom focused our time and conversations on anything more than getting a buzz and having fun. We certainly hadn't discussed the hard parts of life.

I still hadn't told Jayson about my childhood. All he knew was that I didn't have a good relationship with my dad. I hadn't shared stories or memories, mostly out of embarrassment and my deep habit of trying to forget it all.

Jayson's family hadn't been at all like mine, and I feared he wouldn't understand or maybe he wouldn't love someone like me if he knew the truth of how I had lived before we met.

The more I revealed about my childhood to Jayson, the more hurt I felt and the more alarmed he became that this life could even exist for a child. I began to realize all the work I needed to do on my heart. I had never dealt with anything from my past, nor had I forgiven anyone.

For me, the addiction of pretending to forget my past instead of dealing with it would be harder than kicking the addiction of any substance.

I felt reassured as we had these conversations that running from the pain wouldn't make it go away. Every time another memory popped up, I'd relive the same pain. I wasn't moving forward. If I was going to move on, I would need to find a way to forgive instead of pretending to forget.

We were doing a lot of planning at this time, and our conversations drifted from how to prepare our home for a baby to what kind of family we desired to be.

The reality that we were going to be parents, and that it was going to be a huge responsibility, was sinking in.

One day in the summer of 2007, I sent Jayson to talk to our preacher about using the basement of our church for our baby shower. We had continued attending church on most Sundays after our wedding. I still wasn't very interested in the concept, but we were going through the motions, playing the part.

Hours went by as I grew impatient for Jayson to return with the verdict so I could move on with my plans. When he finally burst into the house, the look on his face surprised me. I stood there impatiently, anxious to hear what had happened but angry that it had taken so long, as he began to explain his afternoon.

"Heather, I'm sorry. I know I was supposed to talk to the preacher about the church, but our conversation went in a different direction, and before I knew it, I was in the water getting baptized!"

Jayson had told me he'd been saved as a child. When he was seven years old, he'd felt the urge when the preacher was calling people forward to be saved. Now, the preacher he'd just spent time with had encouraged him to go further, with the act of baptism. I didn't understand any of this, and truthfully, I didn't care.

I was furious as he finished his story with the admission that he hadn't talked to the preacher about the shower at all. Without commenting on his big announcement, I walked away, crying out of selfishness that he hadn't done what I needed him to do.

The whole thing seemed foolish and annoying. I only saw it as him thinking of himself when I really needed him to help. We didn't even talk about it after that.

Sorry, Jayson. I didn't get it.

Our sweet daughter, Savannah Love, was born on August 12, 2007, and of course, our lives changed instantly. That feeling of looking at your baby, realizing you could love someone so much, was amazing. I daydreamed about how we would treat her, how she would come first. She wouldn't have to live the way I had lived. I vowed I would lay down my life to make sure she was happy and felt loved and cared for.

But this also made my own existing hurt cut deep, wondering how a parent could mistreat a precious child, *their* precious child. How could my dad have treated me that way? I had been so innocent, just like our baby girl.

Our lives soon revolved around sweet Savannah. I stayed home and took care of her and the house after her birth while Jayson worked during the day. I adored being a stay-at-home mother, but unfortunately, money was getting tight. I didn't want to get a job and take Savannah to a babysitter, and Jay didn't want that either. So we decided to supplement our income with the talent we shared—music.

When Savannah was about three months old, Jay and I started singing in the evenings at local venues. We made sure that Mom and Mark would be available to watch Savannah while we were planning these gigs. With their assurance that they would help, our music careers began again.

One day as I pushed Savannah in the stroller for her afternoon nap and my afternoon workout, I stopped and perched myself on a bench downtown. I had a phone book, my phone, and a calendar in hand, and I started making cold calls. The first conversation went something like this:

"Hi, my name is Heather Stover. My husband, Jayson, and I play music. He plays acoustic guitar, and we both sing. I was wondering if you would be interested in booking us to play at your bar on a Friday night?"

The owner asked what kind of music we played and how much we charged. I told him we did a variety of rock, country, and some old classics, and that we would charge $250 for three hours of music.

Honestly, it's amazing how easy this was. The bar owner said yes. We booked a Friday without his even hearing us, and we were officially, surprisingly, an acoustic duo ready for tour.

Our act consisted of Jay and me sitting on stools, him playing guitar and both of us singing. We had two music stands that held all the words to our songs, and every now and again I would play the tambourine. That was it.

I was amazed that people were willing to pay us that kind of money to come sit on stools and sing for three hours.

Customers started recommending us to other venues, and not long after we started, we were booking months out in advance. We were making more money than we ever had, and the gigs soon not only filled up our weekends but also our weekdays. We got calls to play in bars and restaurants, which then turned into festivals, private backyard parties, graduation parties, and weddings.

We didn't have a band anymore and decided to go by the name the Stovers. We thought that would make things easy, but oddly enough, we had people criticize this name, saying it sounded like a church group, when we were the furthest thing from it.

Jay was unexpectedly laid off from his job in 2008, which made music our only source of income. It still didn't feel like work though. We had so much fun. Unfortunately, as I got "back to myself" after bearing a child, I began the drinking, smoking, and partying all over again.

Our "work" had become music and parties.

We learned that when you are the entertainment, you drink free—whatever you want, no matter the quantity. I had always naturally been a bit shy and introverted, so when we would show up to our gigs, I made it a routine to take a Patron tequila shot for my nerves. The bartenders soon memorized what I wanted and had it waiting for me no matter the venue. I usually stuck with that and a couple of beers because that was all I could tolerate before I would start forgetting words. Jay, on the other hand, could function with way more alcohol in his system, so he consumed and consumed.

We became well known around our town for a line that we had picked up from another band in Nashville during one of our trips. This was called a "holler and swaller." The "holler," where everyone would scream as loud as they could, and then the "swaller," where we would all chug as much beer or whiskey as we could get down. The more we prompted larger amounts of alcohol, the more the bar owners loved us, and the more they asked us to come back again, as we were increasing their sales.

Other small-town bars outside our hometown caught wind of what we were doing and the new, larger crowds we brought in. The calls for bookings grew. But we didn't comprehend at the time that it wasn't so much because of our music as that they wanted us to lead their customers into greater drunkenness.

By 2010, we were playing on big stages and even got to open for the band Little Texas one night. Maybe you remember their hit song "God Bless Texas"? We played this event even though I was pregnant again. I really didn't want to perform while I was pregnant, but we needed the money. So there I was in a stretched-out Bob Marley T-shirt, shaking a tambourine and dancing away.

We had become big fish in a little bowl, and we were soaking in every minute of small-town fame, but deep down I began to feel the wear of it all on my body and on my mind. And as Savannah got older, I feared her ever seeing us in action.

Two years into playing like this, we started to notice the crowds getting smaller, the praise disappearing, and the feeling of fun evaporating. We weren't getting the compliments we had once received, even though we were singing the same songs. We realized we were getting old. Our music was getting old, and our act was getting even older. We were playing mostly venues and parties that revolved around drinking, and when we couldn't bring the crowds as we once had, the bar owners stopped booking us. This was a huge stress on our family, as we had been relying on that income.

This forced us to say yes to every gig that came our way, which landed us in some uncomfortable situations. Making money with our music during those years took us into some scary situations.

One night at a private party, we realized we'd been hired to play for a group of people leading dogfights. We ended up giving back their money to get out of there unharmed.

Another time, an angry and very intoxicated man made it

known that he had a gun. There we sat onstage in the middle of the venue, planning our escape route and trying not to think of what would become of our two-year-old daughter if something happened to us. I watched the man as he staggered around the bar, resting his hand on the revolver, my fate depending on whether he pulled it out. Talk about feeling helpless.

Luckily, we left that night unharmed.

Then there were the men who hit on me. One evening as we were packing up, an older man came up to me, acting as though he wanted to tell me something. When I leaned over to hear what he was saying, he landed a kiss right on my face and stuck his tongue in my ear.

I thought Jayson might go to jail that night, but when the bar owner came up to us and said, "What do you expect, bringing your wife into a bar like this?" we were speechless. We had no other choice but to acknowledge our own culpability.

People were growing tired of us, and we were exhausted. We tried getting gigs in bigger cities nearby to meet some different people and pretty much start all over again. We were successful in landing the gigs, but we were just another corner act in those places. We were mostly ignored background music, and this shift didn't compare to the praise we were used to getting in the smaller towns.

Sometimes, Jay and I would sing funny words to the songs that were familiar to people to see if anyone was paying attention. They weren't.

One evening, on the way home from a gig that was an hour from home, Jay and I voiced our frustrations about being ignored. Trying to come up with ways to get out of that cycle, I ventured a suggestion.

"You know where we need to play? Church." I kind of

laughed. "Those people might actually listen to us." Then I sat back in my seat and looked out the window. *Where did that come from?*

We had been attending a new church down the road from our house, but we were still pew warmers. We didn't understand anything about God or the Bible at that time. We had just started to feel the conviction of spending our Saturday nights drunk and our Sunday mornings being lazy.

I was surprised at what had come out of my mouth. *What was I thinking? Yeah, go into a church and play our barroom songs.* But it was as if those words had danced out of my mouth without thought or effort, and they hung in the air between us.

Jayson's disgusted look told me he was not impressed with my idea. I knew what he was thinking. Truth be told, so was I. No church would pay us to sing and play for them.

It wouldn't be long, though, before this would all start to make sense. I didn't know it in that car, but God was nudging me—dare I say *pursuing* me? He was giving me thoughts and ideas that I didn't understand.

Have you ever heard it said that the price of forgetting is a life of repetition?

Five years had passed since my dad's death, and over time, the change and wonder I'd experienced had faded. I'd pretty much gone back to the way I'd been living before. It was the only way I knew how to live.

I had started to go to church . . . a little. I tried to be better at life . . . a little. You know, only having a couple of drinks, not being as wild as before. Compared to the life I'd lived previously, these were huge steps, but then I started drifting right back into the old me. And the longer I went on without recognizing my need for a relationship with God, the harder my life got.

Luckily, God wasn't giving up on me.

In 2010, He made Himself known.

I was sitting in my house with three-year-old Savannah, watching a baseball game on TV and eating our regular snack of grapes and popcorn. Jay was out playing a gig. I was pregnant again, so he'd been at it alone in the music business, trying to keep the cash flowing in. We knew it was time for me to stay home when I could no longer fit into my old Bob Marley T-shirt.

Savannah and I were enjoying our snacks, and the Cleveland Indians were up 5–0 when, suddenly, a very active thunderstorm rolled in. The sky turned black as I ran to our second-story window to assess the conditions. Something in me felt different this night at the sound of the thunder, and I was overcome with fear.

Fear at a level I had never known.

I tried to make sense of my feelings as the terror took over my body. I thought maybe my instincts were telling me that this was it, this was the time when our home would be hit by a tornado, like I had seen on the news so many times before. Maybe we should run to the basement. But in that moment, all I could do was stand by the window and look into the dark sky.

The fear that I'd found after my dad's passing reemerged.

The baseball game and snacks were of no importance anymore as old questions began swirling around in my mind. Only this time, they weren't about my dad. They were about me.

Am I going to die tonight?

If I do, where will I go?

Sadly, I didn't have any answers.

Looking out the bedroom window at the black sky, I thought, *What if this is it? What if Jesus is coming now?*

I had listened enough in church over the past few years to hear a lot about this event and that it was going to happen at some point.

Preachers would often talk about the return of Jesus, but usually I sat there, void of feeling, thinking, *Yeah, that's not going to happen for a long time.*

But this night, it became real, and I cared.

> Look, I am coming soon! My reward is with me, and I will give to each person according to what they have done.
> Revelation 22:12 NIV

I knew I wasn't saved. I didn't have a secure eternity. I hadn't humbled myself to accept Jesus's existence; I'd never even admitted I needed saving. I was still living in victim mode and hadn't acknowledged that I had sins of my own.

I had pridefully shrugged away all the Christian talk before now, but for some reason, this day I was terrified. Tears filled my eyes as I stared out into the storm.

Fearfully looking to the sky where I had kept God for so long, I mouthed a desperate plea. *Please help me!*

Inside, I thought, *This is it. I'm done. I can't live like this anymore.* I had to know where I would go if I died and where my dad went when he died. I was learning and being convicted that I had to quit running from my past and start running to God. Nothing else made sense.

As Savannah sat on my bed watching, her mouth full of popcorn, I prayed the best I knew how. I prayed a simple prayer, not fully understanding what I was doing. Aloud, I said, "Please save me, God."

The next day, I called the pastor of the church we were attending at the time and asked if I could come in to talk with him. He agreed to meet me that afternoon. I didn't tell Jayson or anyone else what was going on or what had happened, but I couldn't get myself to that pastor's office quickly enough.

I walked into his office, with Savannah holding my hand and toddling beside me. I had on a black maternity dress that fell just below the knee. Suddenly I realized my ankle tattoo was showing, and I panicked. *Oh no, he's going to see my tattoo.* Good Christian people didn't have tattoos, did they?

Ugh.

I just knew he was going to think I was terrible. But I had desperation flowing through my veins. I was again acting like another preacher would be God himself, but this time I was worried he would judge *me*.

He didn't. He had a twinkle in his eye as I told him what had happened. I explained that I didn't know why, but I felt like I needed to be baptized, urgently.

He explained that in that church, there was a process to become a member, then I could be baptized. He added that the baptisms were done in front of the congregation. I was not too thrilled about that, but the urgency was real. I agreed, willing to do whatever was necessary.

We set a day for Savannah and me to be baptized, because I figured I might as well do the work for her too.

I know now, so don't get mad if you're reading this and thinking, *Oh my goodness. She has no idea what she's talking about. She doesn't know anything about the gospel!* You're right; I didn't know then. I didn't understand that I had already been saved when I prayed that prayer in the bedroom. I had acknowledged that I believed in God and pleaded with Him to save me. But I didn't understand what I had done that night. I also didn't know that baptism is not a requirement for salvation or to get into heaven. I was navigating my way through this process the best I could.

Truth was, I had been saved the moment I'd acknowledged God and my belief in His power.

> And everyone who calls on the name of the Lord will be saved.
> Acts 2:21 NIV

I had been saved when I asked God for salvation that night. There were no further acts needed on my part, but conviction was consuming me and urging me to get baptized so that if Jesus came back in the next storm, I would know where I was going.

The first Sunday morning after the intense storm, Savannah and I were baptized. Pregnant with our second child, I stood before the congregation being sprinkled with water and prayed over, then Savannah took her turn, not having a clue what she was doing either. She sucked quietly on her pacifier, her big blue eyes looking at me while what I thought was her salvation water dripped down her nose.

For the longest time after this, I thought that baptism was it. I had gained my ticket to heaven. I was good to go. Life would be smooth sailing from then on.

Thank You, Jesus, for time and patience. God was pursuing me, but my eyes were not yet open to see the full picture of the gospel, and my ears were not in tune to hear the truth when it was taught.

One thing was apparent though. God was in the process of transforming my heart.

Chapter Seven

Finding the Holy Spirit in Florida

Jayson and I had our second child, Noah Jay, on February 9, 2011.

Noah was born with wavy red hair. At eight pounds two ounces, he seemed half grown when he entered the world. With Noah's inherited facial features, red hair, and blue eyes, I saw my dad every time I looked at him. My heart softened as I wondered what life would have been like if my dad hadn't been an addict and how he might have been with my children if he had been able to meet them. Noah brought back thoughts of the other side of my family that I had stored away.

Jayson's parents had moved to Florida in 2007, weeks after Savannah was born. We were not thrilled that they were moving right after the birth of their first grandchild, but we were intrigued at the thought of moving somewhere new with them.

We visited them a couple of times in Florida and thought it looked glamorous and full of opportunity. We knew that if we moved there too, our music might flourish, and we could potentially make something more of our talents.

We decided we would try. Jay and I started selling our large possessions and began to save and plan for the move.

By the time Noah turned six months old and Savannah was about to turn four, we grew impatient. All we could think about was the sand between our toes and the warmth of the sun on our skin. We talked about the ocean and the beautiful sunsets we longed to see. We knew we could stay with Jay's parents until we figured things out. So we jumped the gun without the right amount of money or planning and took out a loan to get there.

In August 2011, I boarded a plane for Florida with my two young children. Jayson was finishing up the packing and would drive one of our cars and meet us the next day. The moving truck containing our belongings had already started its journey to Florida by the time we were on the plane.

We arrived at the Tampa airport and waited for my father-in-law to pick us up. I had Noah in a car seat, Savannah on a backpack leash, and my carry-on bag. My father-in-law greeted us by placing a lei around Savannah's and my necks and a small flower anklet around Noah's ankle. As if we had arrived on a dream vacation in Hawaii.

Reality started to sink in as we walked out of the airport together. I was so uncomfortable experiencing all this without Jayson. I wanted to cry, but I couldn't. I had to act happy to match my colorful lei.

We had done it. We had given up everything we knew.

Our home, familiar people, good friends, my newly rekindled relationship with my mom, and comfort.

I had landed in another corner of the country without my husband, without a car, without any of my possessions—other than what I could fit in a book bag—and without return tickets. We had no jobs, no home, and no idea what we were going to do.

As if all that reality weren't enough, as soon as we made it to my in-laws' house, both of the kids spiked fevers.

Oh yeah, and no doctor.

Realizing you've made a huge mistake as soon as you make it is humbling. And in this case, slightly terrifying.

The plan was to stay with Jayson's parents until he found a job, then find our own place to rent. Our focus, though, was playing music in bigger, nicer beachfront venues.

Even with all our savings and planning, the personal loan we had taken out had a crazy interest rate, and our monthly payment was huge. We thought the loan would be enough to take care of our needs until we got on our feet, but we didn't understand the highly inflated cost of living in Florida and how hard this was going to be.

When Jayson arrived the next day, I was relieved to see him and tried to pretend I felt good about what we had done. But it had already sunk in. We had messed up.

Jayson soon joined me in these thoughts, and the nightmare began.

There we were with two small children, living in the two extra bedrooms Jay's parents had. Other than our belongings that were stashed inside his parents' two-car garage, all we had were no jobs and a pile of debt.

Looking back, our reason for making this move is fuzzy. I know we thought the grass would be greener. We would have the ocean, the beach, and the sun all the time! What we were not prepared for was the drastic change in lifestyle and the consequences of ungratefulness for what we had given up.

After the initial shock, it started to feel kind of like a vacation. We were in a beautiful home with palm trees everywhere we looked. We were a short drive from the beach, and the sun was shining every morning when we opened our eyes. But after a few weeks, the vacation feels were gone, and reality began to creep back in.

Jayson found a job doing construction, but we hadn't realized that good-paying jobs in Ohio were not good-paying jobs in Florida. This did not align well with the fact that the cost of living in Florida was way higher than in Ohio. Jayson was ready to move back within the first month of working outside during a Florida summer. I was too, but I never told him. I knew we couldn't afford to move back. Our finances were now terrible.

We were stuck!

The stress from the move, motherly duties, and Savannah starting preschool caused me more anxiety than I had ever known. I would drop Savannah off at preschool in the mornings, go back to my in-laws' house to clean up any messes we had made, feed Noah, and then sleep. I couldn't get enough sleep, which I soon learned is a common symptom of anxiety and depression. Luckily, Noah enjoyed napping for long periods, so this worked.

I slept all the time because when I wasn't sleeping, I was panicking. I had started having severe panic attacks. I saw a doctor who prescribed medication, but now I felt like a crazy person. I had so much anxiety that I couldn't even take a single pill, which, looking back, I'm glad I never started. But that doesn't mean I didn't clinically meet the criteria.

I would sit alone at the house, feeling my arms and legs go numb (another symptom). My heart raced, and I soon started having cold sweats. I let worry consume my days, fearful that I was going to pass out and Noah would be alone. I called Jayson frequently at work and told him I was going to call an ambulance because I knew I was dying. He didn't have any sympathy for me. He was miserable himself. He told me it was all in my head and that I needed to get it together. He couldn't come home from work early to be with me.

Tough love.

He was right. I did need to get it together, but my insides were out of control. Some of the feelings I developed in Florida brought back the feelings I had as a child, and at times I fought the urge to go to the mirror to find what I always thought would be waiting.

We knew we had to make the best of the situation, so Jayson worked hard, I held it together somehow, and we eventually found a nice rental home. We used our personal loan to pay for the first six months' rent. But we soon realized that in Jayson's line of work, he was not going to make enough money for us to continue living in the house. When we had to start paying the personal loan payments with money from the personal loan, we knew we were in trouble. Jayson and I had been used to financial stress, but never to this degree.

We decided, after running the numbers, that it would be better if I went to work instead of Jay. We were still determined that we would not have a daily babysitter in our lives. I had switched majors four times but had finally finished my degree in 2010 with a bachelor's degree in business administration. Of course, the number of credits I had earned was probably enough to become a doctor, but I still had no idea what I wanted to do.

With my credentials, it was easy to land a job in a medical office in Sarasota. I liked my job, and apparently, I was doing well because in only one month, the CFO brought in the CEO to meet me. These people were all business and loved the money I had been able to bring in working with patients' financial accounts.

The day the CEO came to meet me, I was sitting in my office. He walked up and shook my hand, then asked me a little bit about myself and where my family had come from. I explained briefly how we had moved from Ohio with no plan, not knowing what was going to happen. I'll never forget what this man said to me.

He looked me square in the eyes and said, "Wow. To leave your home and move across the country with no job and no place of your own really takes a big faith."

Faith.

That word caught my attention.

I thought about it long and hard that day. We hadn't been to a church since the move. In fact, God's name hadn't even been mentioned, and our Bibles were boxed up somewhere.

Do Jay and I really have faith, like he said? Do we really have faith that everything is going to be okay here?

No. We might have appeared to have faith, but we were impostors. We had jumped and left everything we knew for sunny weather and the dream that someone important would hear our music and give us our "big break." We were seeking the praise of people. Our desire to be known had blinded our common sense. We hadn't appreciated the comfort that we'd had in Ohio.

The reality was that we were miserable. I had gone from being a stay-at-home mom taking care of my babies to a full-time businesswoman. Jayson was now the stay-at-home dad, running the household like a construction site. These were not roles that suited either of us, but we were doing our best to pretend because we were too prideful to admit we had messed up.

Family and friends would call from Ohio. We'd lie, boasting about how wonderful the weather was and how much we loved our new house. We skimmed over the fact that we hated the heat and that most days were so hot we couldn't even go outside. We didn't mention the reality that snakes and fire ants were a threat every time we walked out the door, or that frogs and lizards would sneak into our house and cause pure chaos.

No, we would only talk about the good parts, or make the things that should have been good *sound* good. Like the fact that we had palm trees in our front yard and that we could go to the beach anytime we wanted. The truth was, we didn't have time to go to the beach or any extra money to have fun.

Within a couple months of living in this new "beach paradise," we were back onstage, trying once again to make more money. Jay and I sang songs to the tourists on Siesta Key every weekend while his parents kept the kids. During the week, we played music on Anna Maria Island to the tourists after I worked my nine-to-five.

We watched these tourists as they drank and enjoyed their families. I remember observing the multiple bags of cherished souvenirs hanging from their arms. I grew more and more jealous of the fact that they had plane tickets home. They'd be walking around snapping pictures on their phones, filling them with memories they could take back with them and applauding the songs we were singing over and over. Meanwhile, we could barely pay our bills.

Palm trees were our background, ocean breezes filled the air, and all the drunk vacationers loved us.

We were exhausted!

Other musicians joined us sometimes. One guy sat on a box with cymbals taped to his hands and feet. He was so amusing to me that I nearly forgot to sing my parts. Another man named

Duckie, who was semi-impressed with our musical abilities, sat in and played drums for us on our best-paying gigs.

There were times when I was so completely exhausted from working all day, then changing clothes in the bathroom, that I would doze off or forget the words. Duckie, even on the "girl songs," would keep it going, because he knew the words by heart. He had been doing this far longer than we had. This was how he made his living; this was his turf. But he didn't have a family. He had a van, a set of drums, and an appetite for alcohol and the nightlife.

Jay decided to use his time at home during the week to work on a CD that he had always dreamed of creating with the songs he'd written. He set up shop in the garage attached to our house and spent countless hours recording every instrument to his original songs.

Although I knew he loved our children and was making sure their basic needs were met, I worried that he was spending so much time on music that it wasn't fair to them. This was not the life I wanted for our kids. We were so busy trying to make ends meet that we were losing each other and our family unity.

We were living the family life *and* the nightlife, and I couldn't take it anymore.

I felt like we had done what we came to do. But like most things in life, it didn't fill us with all the happiness we thought it would. We had made the move. We had gotten jobs. We lived in the house with palm trees in the front yard, minutes from some of the most beautiful beaches in the world. We had easily landed gigs in some of the hottest tourist spots in the state.

But none of it was fulfilling.

We realized we had gone from being big fish in a little bowl to little fish in a big bowl. These tourist attractions were not hurting for entertainers who would sit for four or more hours at a time, strumming their guitars and singing their hearts out in the scorching heat.

We were yet again a living jukebox on the good days and background music on the bad. But we were always going to be there for *them*. No one was going to be there for *us*.

I also realized at this time that Jayson was developing a drinking problem. I think it took me so long to understand that he really had a problem because alcohol had always been a part of our lives. But the more music we played and the more free drinks we consumed, the bigger the problem became.

Jayson had built up quite a tolerance and could function well with high amounts of alcohol, but it was affecting his attitude toward me. I noticed him spiraling out of control with his consumption of alcohol, and I backed away. I confronted him occasionally about what he was doing, but it only made him angry. And I wasn't in any condition to deal with someone else's addictions.

There came a time in this beautiful Florida home when Jay and I didn't even sleep in the same room. I'll be honest—I got to a point where I couldn't stand being around him. He was different. He had let the stress of this move and the pressure of trying to do something with his gift of music weigh him down. The weight from all the pressure to succeed was changing him. And it wasn't a good change.

As I backed away from the nightlife and encouraged him to play gigs by himself, we grew further apart. I relished the fact that I could come home from work like a normal mother and spend time with my then four-year-old and one-year-old babies. I felt like I had already missed so much. The satisfaction I had once felt from the attention of the spotlight was gone. I just wanted to hide and be with my children.

What I didn't realize then was that when I had prayed that prayer during the thunderstorm, my soul had begun to change, because I had been filled with the Holy Spirit. Desires and addictions were being removed. But that didn't mean the change would be quick. I didn't know what God had in store for us until I finally hit my breaking point.

A year into living in Florida, after a heated argument about moving home, Jayson left in a fit of rage, saying there was no way he was going to admit failure and move back. As the kids napped, I sat on our couch looking out the window at a neighborhood that was still foreign to me. I looked up at the sky where I was still keeping God and again whispered, "Please help me."

I had been thinking about leaving Jayson.

I still loved him, but I didn't like the person he had become, and I was not going to allow my children to suffer a childhood with unhappy parents and addiction, like I had.

As I tried to figure out what to do, I felt God's answer. I didn't understand how I knew it was God. Maybe faith? But words to a song started playing in my mind. A song I had never heard. I realized this was not yet a song at all, but a song for me, from God. I was amazed at the words He was giving me. Everything I had been feeling and couldn't make sense of since we'd moved started to be clear as the words played in my mind.

Would these words make sense to Jayson?

Almost as soon as the thought came to mind, I knew the answer.

Of course! This is the only way Jayson will listen to me. A song!

I grabbed a pen and paper and wrote down the words God had given me. It started out as a letter to Jayson, explaining how I felt and that I so longed to go home. Then as the melody played in my mind, the words poured out.

I'll admit I get a fix, going out and playing these old
smokey late-night gigs.
You and me, up on stage, seeing how much praise
and money we can raise,
but as we live it up and take all this small-town fame in,
we're missing little things that make our children grin.

(Chorus)

Oh, time and that dollar sign
are really gonna make me lose my mind.
I'm running out of both of them
and at the same time, I'm losing all my family and
my friends.
I'm trying hard to keep on keeping on with my faith,
but I can't deny I'm seeing myself break.
There's a life I see in my head
but it breaks me every day I have, to tuck it in and
pretend.
I can feel my heart start to drown
as I think about the broken roads in our small hometown.
Take me back to where I felt the love and where who
I was would always be enough.

(Chorus)

I don't know which way to go; should I keep on
trying for what you want, or should I just go home?
I can't count on anything in this life,
but I can make my own happiness and go on with
my life.
I don't know what you really even want
and if you get it will it be enough

The song poured out of my soul, and I felt relieved, as I knew this would touch Jayson and he would be intrigued that it had been done as music.

When he returned, I told him I had written a song. He was taken aback by this statement because, well, I had never written a song. But he was equally excited, since that was what he lived for at that time in our life. He grabbed his guitar and began to strum as I hummed the melody God had given me. Despite the fact that I was still mad and frustrated at how he'd been acting, this song seemed to end the argument. Without much effort from us, the song "Time" was born.

With it came serious discussion about what we should do. We both knew we needed to make a change of some sort. We couldn't keep living the way we were.

Financial issues and pride weighed heavy in both of our minds, but we also shared intense feelings of failure. We began throwing out questions, trying to figure out what to do.

"Can we afford to move home?"

"Where would we live?"

"What about schools?"

"Savannah loves her school. How is she going to feel about moving again?"

"If we move home," I blurted out, "I can homeschool the kids."

Those words hung in the air between us, just like they had when I'd suggested the crazy idea of playing music at church.

I shut my mouth and just stared at Jayson, who shared my shock at what I had said. We had never discussed the option of homeschooling. We didn't know anyone who homeschooled or who had been homeschooled.

All I could think of while I stared at my husband and confirmed with a nod that I meant what I'd said was, *Why in the world did I say that?*

I was freaking out in my mind because of the look on Jayson's face. This would be the deciding factor in moving home. I felt in that moment, sitting in the living room of our Florida home, that something more than me was speaking. I had started feeling like God was speaking to me, because I had never before experienced the voice I was now hearing within. But I didn't know enough to realize that the words that kept flying out of my mouth in random moments were from the Holy Spirit.

Understanding the Holy Spirit can be a lifelong journey of searching and learning, but it's so exciting when you get a glimpse of what—or rather, *who*—the Holy Spirit is.

I love the way it's explained in my NKJV *Women's Study Bible*. This version says that the Holy Spirit is the third person of the Trinity and thus should be referenced as "He," not "it" (John 14:17; 15:26; 16:7, 13):

> He possesses all God's attributes and is fully God. Throughout history, God has acted, revealed His will, empowered individuals, and disclosed His personal presence through the Holy Spirit.
>
> The Holy Spirit has specific functions. In the Old Testament, the Holy Spirit was given to an individual at a specific time to aid in accomplishing a particular assignment or mission (Numbers 11:26, Ezekiel 2:2). He was not constantly present in the life of every follower of Yahweh (God). However, from the coming of the Spirit in the New Testament until Jesus return the end of the (Church) Age, the Holy Spirit indwells all believers from the moment they trust completely in the Lord and His saving power.
>
> When an individual accepts Jesus as Savior, the Holy Spirit comes to indwell, never to leave (Ephesians 4:30 [& 1:13–14]). The Holy Spirit is the believer's greatest asset (or *gift)* and is essential

for survival in this sinful world. The Holy Spirit is the believer's advocate (John 14:16). In other words, the Holy Spirit is "Comforter" and "Teacher" (John 16:7, 13). The Holy Spirit gives the believer help and advice for living the Christian life.

As moment-by-moment believers surrender their lives to God and allow themselves to be used for God's service, the filling of the Holy Spirit occurs. Through the filling of the Holy Spirit, believers are controlled by the Spirit and equipped for service (Ephesians 5:18–21, Romans 12, Spiritual gifts; 2 Cor. 1, Conscience; Eph. 5; God's Will, 1 Peter 2).[1]

I didn't know all of that yet, but it dawned on me in that moment that, when I was saved, I really had been *changed*. It would take some time for me to understand fully, but I felt that the Holy Spirit was not only guiding me but was a part of me. He was in me!

The decision was made. We were moving back to Ohio.

---

1 NKJV *Women's Study Bible, New King James version* (Thomas Nelson, 1982), 1608.

Chapter Eight

Licking Wounds

I had to shove my pride into my pocket and make a phone call to Mamaw, who had told us that moving to Florida was a bad idea in the first place. I knew she was the only one who could and would help us financially.

I could feel my throat closing as I forced the words out. I told her I needed to get away from Florida. That if we stayed, my marriage wouldn't last, and I was experiencing anxiety like I never had before. I explained that I was having panic attacks all the time, and tears would not stop falling from my exhausted eyes.

Ever since Mamaw and I had formed our relationship, she had been my saving grace whenever I didn't have enough. Enough love, enough food, enough wisdom, and this time—like many others—enough money. She didn't hesitate when I told her we needed to come home.

She didn't say "I told you so" or "Why didn't you listen to me?"

She simply said, with love and excitement, "How much do you need?"

This was no easy twenty-dollar fix. We needed money for a U-Haul and four plane tickets. We figured that the cost of moving would be well over three thousand dollars, just to get our stuff and our bodies back to Ohio.

And we needed to move our family of four *in with her*.

Lovingly, Mamaw put a check in the mail that day.

In September 2012, my family and I moved back from Florida.

We were excited and relieved to get home, but the stress was heavy. As Jayson described it, we would be "licking our wounds" for a long time. We had racked up substantial debt trying to live comfortably in a foreign land, and we had no house to go home to.

But we made it back to Ohio.

We decided that our best bet would be to move our things to a storage unit while living with Mamaw, who had a big enough house for us to stay until we found a place of our own. She was so kind, but I felt terrible bringing my baggage into her home again. All four of us moved into the same bedroom I had once occupied by myself.

Jayson found a job the same week we moved back, and I was able to work remotely for the company I had worked for in Florida—but that left me no time to homeschool. So despite the Holy Spirit's prompting not to, I enrolled my then five-year-old in kindergarten.

Not surprisingly, this turned out to be a terrible idea. She lasted about three weeks in public school before we noticed something was not right.

Savannah had been in preschool in Florida and had been fine, but going to kindergarten was a different story. Our inconsistency and rambling around had affected her more than I thought it would. She cried every single day, all day, and then into the night as well. She'd wake in the mornings with swollen eyes and no smile in sight. She looked awful. She acted depressed. And I was at my wit's end.

You know the scene when a young child cries and throws a fit at the thought of school? This usually happens before the child gets out of the car or as the parent is walking them into the building. This was not the case here. Savannah kept her head lowered as slow tears streamed down her face. There was no fight. Only pure disappointment at the fact that she had to walk into the building. Every day. I felt terrible.

Finally, when I couldn't take my mama-hurts anymore, I decided I would let her stay home for a couple of days to try to figure out what we should do. How could we get our five-year-old to be happy again? I felt really convicted that we were just dragging these babies around while we chased our own dreams. I realized how unfair it was to them. Savannah was old enough now that I could see the effect our problems were having on her, and it broke my heart.

One evening as I was getting ready for bed in my grandmother's large bathroom, Savannah came in. I'll never forget the look on her face. She was crying as she slid down to the floor, as if she were too weak to remain upright.

"Savannah," I said, "you're going to have to try to enjoy school and make some friends."

She stuck out her lip. "Not at this school."

I didn't understand. "Is there a reason you don't like this school?"

Her baby blues locked with mine, and with the most serious tone a five-year-old could muster, she said, "Please just give me a chance."

Her words startled me as they hung in the air, just as my own words had been doing recently. "What are you talking about?"

Her reply was even more startling. "Please give me a chance with homeschool."

Savannah was only five, and we had never spoken with her about this idea. How could she know what that even meant?

Something about her seemed different as she spoke. It was like she had a wisdom to her and a glow in her eye that I had never seen before. I knew for sure in that moment that God was speaking straight to me through the mouth of my child. Had Savannah received the Holy Spirit as well?

I couldn't hold back the tears. "Okay, we can try this thing together."

Then I watched my baby smile for the first time in a long time.

I would later confirm that God was absolutely speaking through the mouth of a child, because we did it, and somehow it worked. We took Savannah out of school and declared ourselves to be homeschoolers for her kindergarten year, knowing absolutely nothing about homeschooling.

That decision to homeschool out of obedience to the Holy Spirit was the one decision that completely wrecked our lives in all the best ways. The Holy Spirit had spoken through me to my husband with this idea, and then confirmation came through my daughter to me. Living in one bedroom at my grandmother's house was not the ideal place to start this new venture, but it felt right.

I took some time after pulling Savannah out of school to research homeschooling. As the kids took their afternoon naps, I would quietly open my laptop and search. Shockingly, everything I looked up about homeschooling pointed to Jesus. There was scripture about raising up your children in the way that they should go, and about how it was our job to teach our children.

I was amazed and encouraged at all I was finding. I began writing down scripture for the first time in my life as inspiration to teach Savannah—and also to convince myself that I

> Train up a child in the way he should go and when he is old, he will not depart from it.
> Proverbs 22:6 KJV

had made the right choice. I bought some materials I thought I needed. I got her curriculum figured out, then started teaching her to read.

It didn't take long before doubt and frustration emerged. I became convinced that I was doing Savannah a huge disservice, as I had no idea how others did it. Savannah had no friends to play with, and Jayson was always working or playing music, trying to get us out of debt and out of Mamaw's house. That left me with little support in the parenting department.

During this season, my two children and I spent our days in the one bedroom we shared at my grandmother's home with two beds, one TV, and a computer.

Finally, a few weeks into homeschooling, I pulled up an internet search page and typed in "homeschooling support." The first thing that popped up on my screen was a link to a school I had never heard of but that was literally thirty minutes from where I had lived most of my life.

I clicked on the link and began reading. It was a school for pre-K through twelfth grade, and guess what? They had a program where kids could be homeschooled but get to go to school a couple of Fridays a month. As I read on, I learned that they provided services in curriculum and instruction, plus academic and biblical resources, along with a monthly home visit to ensure success.

I was giddy with excitement and relief, thinking this was exactly what I needed, until it sank in that this was a private Christian school that would cost money to attend. And then it all made sense. That was exactly the reason I had never heard of it before. I didn't know anyone who had ever attended a Christian school.

But I called the number and spoke to an incredibly kind woman. I truly would describe this experience as being guided by angels, because the lady was helpful and gave me so much peace. She answered my questions and understood when I told her I was lost in the idea of homeschooling. I blurted out in excitement that I thought God was leading my family in this direction, and I knew I had to try it.

She emailed the information to me that day, and I let her know I would look everything over and get back with her if I was still interested.

Only a week after typing that question into that search engine, I found myself attending a meeting at a local coffee shop with other homeschooling moms. The woman on the phone had given me information about these meetings in case I wanted to meet some families from the school.

Truth be told, I felt like a complete fraud walking into the building. I wasn't like these people. I didn't read the Bible much. I didn't have any scripture memorized, and we hadn't been to church since before we had moved to Florida. I didn't know any other Christians and didn't know the language or how to pray out loud, and honestly, I wasn't even comfortable talking about God. I didn't really know Him yet.

I felt awkward joining in on the conversation, so I only listened. These women didn't know it, but they were teaching me what it meant and looked like to not only be a homeschooling mom but to be a Christian. I had never had personal relationships with Christians, so sitting in a coffee shop full of them was a bit overwhelming.

The conversation was fascinating. They didn't talk about partying or work. They didn't gossip. Instead, pure encouragement came from every one of their mouths. They prayed together and talked about what God was doing in their lives and how He was helping them. They seemed genuinely curious about me and made me feel wanted and loved.

They had no idea I had just moved home from Florida and had spent years playing music in bars. They certainly had no idea I was the product of a broken home or that I had addictions of my own that I was overcoming. I kept quiet and took in every bit that I could from these women. Then I drove home to Mamaw's house, trying to make sense of everything they had said and smiling as I sat by myself in the car. For the first time ever, I felt uplifted and encouraged by faithful women.

I had begun researching the idea of reading the Bible, only because I had begun researching homeschooling, and those passages about parenting had grown more wonder in my heart. I desired to be a good parent. I wanted to make my children feel more love than I had as a child. I wanted to be there for them and for them to know they were important to me and deserved to be cherished.

But I still battled the unforgiveness that tortured my heart, the self-pity that weighed on me daily from my own childhood, and a growing certainty that there must be another way to live. I realized this way of life wasn't something I could do on my own, because in many ways, I was still just like a child. Feeling small and lost, and longing for something more than this world had to offer.

I needed to be taught myself before I could teach them.

We put church on our calendar for Sunday mornings, and this school began to feel like the only one that would work for our family. One thing became crystal clear after witnessing this other way of life. The church, the Bible, God, and now this school were necessary if we were really going to change.

After attending a couple of these meetings, I made an appointment to talk with the homeschooling principal to see about getting Savannah into the program for her first-grade year.

Still living at my grandma's, we went to church one Sunday—the same church where Savannah and I had been baptized. Then we went the next week and the next and the next, until soon we became regulars. Jayson went too, even though he was often hungover. I'll give him credit. He did have the desire to be with me and the kids, so he pushed through.

These people knew us from around town as the barroom singers—after all, we lived in a village where everyone knew everyone else—yet they still welcomed us in. We found ourselves going out to dinner with other members of the church, and I started volunteering to help in the nursery. We were becoming a part of this church family as we watched and learned more about what it meant to be a Christian.

More importantly, I was learning *that I was one.*

In that church building, we started experiencing the love of God through His people, and the desire to know Him deeper.

I continued homeschooling Savannah on my own through kindergarten while still attending the support group at the coffee shop and church every Sunday morning, all while attempting to feel less like a fraud.

The summer before Savannah entered first grade, I interviewed again with the school to see if we were good enough to get into the Christian homeschooling program. There was an extensive application process to get our child accepted, and I feared we were not going to make the cut. They researched our church attendance, called our pastor, and asked us to write about where we stood on our beliefs. We admitted that we were new to this but felt like God had led us there.

To my delight, we made the cut and were advised that a teacher would be at our house to check on Savannah's academic progress periodically. We still lived in that single bedroom on the second floor of Mamaw's house, and the urgency to move out increased. We needed to set up a school space for Savannah in a place of our own.

As we progressed on our journey, things were changing, and they were good. I felt good, as my anxiety had started to subside, and we had a plan. I would continue to homeschool Savannah and work remotely for the company in Sarasota, while being home with Noah full time until the next school year started. I looked forward to receiving the support and guidance from the school that I was desperately seeking. This couldn't have been more perfect!

Things were looking up for me and the kids, but Jayson was mostly gone.

He had grown even more angry since we'd moved back to Ohio. Life got more overwhelming for him because of our living situation and our finances. He worked around the clock, which was exhausting. I didn't know how to help him as my plate was already full, but our relationship was falling apart.

When we had saved enough money for a deposit, we began looking for houses to rent. We found a Victorian home that had been made into a triplex, only a block from Mamaw's house. It was almost directly across the street from the first home that Jayson and I had owned.

It was hard looking at our first house as we stood in the front yard of this Victorian home. That was the home where I had grieved for my dad, where we'd come after our honeymoon, and where Savannah had spent her infancy. Talk about going full circle.

When we walked through the back door of the triplex, I knew that this would be our new home.

I thought it was marvelous. It was huge! There was an upstairs unit with two bedrooms and one bath; a main floor unit with two bedrooms and one bath; and a very small one-bedroom, one-bath unit in the basement. The whole house had a gorgeous wraparound porch enclosed by windows from top to bottom.

I loved this place. It had so much character and was spotless. There were giant heavy wooden hideaway doors and a beautiful antique fireplace in one of the bedrooms of the main floor unit. We earnestly decided we wanted that apartment!

The owner was a German man in his late seventies. John was very particular, fit, and neatly dressed. We could tell he took pride in this old house as he explained that he had owned it for over forty years. We followed him around as he showed us bit by bit all the work he had personally done to make it unique.

He and Jayson hit it off, and he was so kind and tolerant of our two very small children, who were running around exploring his masterpiece. The men ended up conversing about man stuff, which left me to wander around by myself. I looked up at the ceilings, which were higher than any I had ever seen, then admired the porch with its inviting swing, where I imagined reading to the kids on sunny afternoons. I couldn't wait to have our own place again.

We were excited that all the units were currently empty. John said that if we moved in now, we would have the house to ourselves at least for a little while. We agreed this would be great for our immediate needs and started the paperwork.

There was one problem though. Our credit was still bad from the move. It didn't look like we were going to pass the financial inspection that this meticulous man had requested. He was working with a real estate agent to make sure only stable tenants would move into the house. We were the furthest thing from stable.

We filled out the application anyway.

As we all sat at the real estate office, waiting on the verdict, the agent looked at John with a raised brow.

"I say no." He pinched his lips together. "They're a risk!"

We were so let down and embarrassed when we heard this news. What were we going to do?

Much to our surprise, however, John had seen something else. He saw a family with two young children who needed a home. He let us move in anyway, explaining that, for some reason, he trusted us.

We rented the main floor with the giant hideaway doors in the biggest bedroom. We ended up putting all three beds there, since everyone had gotten so used to sharing a room.

Savannah started her year of independent studies at the Christian school in August 2014. We have a picture of her in her uniform complete with a red polo shirt, navy skirt, and pink sparkly Sperrys, standing in front of the lime-green walls of the apartment. She looked so much happier. She loved being home but eventually looked forward to those special days each month when she could go to the school with other students her age and teachers other than her mom.

I felt better with my anxiety, and I think Noah enjoyed being with his mama again. I certainly cherished my time with him. But Jayson and I were not communicating and seemed more like roommates than a couple. He was still working a full-time job and had started a small business on the side building snowplow trucks, still working tirelessly to get us out of debt.

He worked all day, came home to eat, then rushed back out to the shop to build trucks. He was always angry and tired, which made me avoid any type of conversation with him. When he did have time off, he wanted to unwind and enjoy his passion in life—playing guitar—which was accompanied by alcohol. This usually led him down the road to the old familiar bars we used to hang out in, where people paid him to drink and sing.

The stress and lack of communication continued to threaten our marriage. We were excited to have found a place of our own and were getting over the process of licking the wounds from our mistakes in Florida, but our relationship was far from healthy.

John had let us move in by the grace of God, but our problems were real, and we could barely afford even this simple life. We knew deep down there was no end in sight with the debt, but we kept trying, paying every bit we could to climb out of the pit of debt we owed.

Because of the unresolved stress, Jay and I reached a point where we couldn't stand to even look at one another. He eventually took the second bedroom in the apartment, which worked out nicely because it was right by the bathroom, kitchen, and outside door. As long as I stayed on my half of the apartment until he was gone, peace could remain.

Jay's drinking and anger had taken a toll on our relationship. I found myself despising the music, the thing that had brought us together. The innocence and joy with which we had once sung our songs and played our instruments had turned into a sinful drunken lifestyle that I no longer wanted, and our marriage felt as though it was coming to an end.

I had no desire to go to bars anymore. I didn't want to sing, and I didn't want to dance and perform as we had done for all those years. I didn't need the attention or want to be in the spotlight. I just wanted to be home with my babies.

Unfortunately, there were some venues that would only book us if it was both of us as a duo. Knowing I couldn't take that money away from the family, I went. I knew I had to continue, even though my heart was hardening more and more toward Jayson and the music itself.

Being a mother was the biggest blessing in my life. I felt most alive when I could be a mom and wife, but Jay couldn't share these feelings with me, as he carried the weight of our mistakes and had taken on full responsibility for making things right again.

He had real musical talent and a strong drive to make something happen with it, but nothing seemed to be working. His dreams had become a hindrance in our lives. A regular nine-to-five was no longer an option in his mind because that meant he'd be wasting his talent, but "making it" by the world's standards now seemed impossible.

Jay would frequently bust through the apartment in anger, going from job to job or job to gig. Communication was so absent from our lives that I got to a point where I didn't know if he was working or playing music. I never knew where he was and became not only bitter about the music, but also bitter toward my husband.

Jayson became reckless with his habits, and other people started to notice. Some nights, he would laugh and tell me about how he had gotten away from the cops, as if this was a rush that he welcomed.

I didn't think it was funny.

One night, after he'd gotten away from the police while

driving drunk, he seriously looked me in the eye and told me that he was special and that they would never get him. I had nothing to say to this. All I could do was stare because I had no strength left to fight the fight that he was always looking for.

Although I was playing the part of Christian homeschooling mom—cooking, cleaning, mothering, teaching, and attending church—our home was far from what a Christian home should be. Jayson's problem with alcohol came into the home, fighting was still our biggest form of communication, and I was losing hope for a change in Jayson.

Then one night, like many others, Jay flew out the back door, angry and looking for somewhere to go drink his problems away. He stumbled down the road and noticed that there was partying going on at the home of a neighbor we didn't know. He walked up to the house and started conversing with some people on the porch.

This is typical Jayson. He could have a good conversation with a wall. He ended up going inside the house, toward the things he was always seeking: alcohol, loud music, and what he called "something to do."

As he drank and talked to these new people, they brought out drugs that he wasn't interested in.

He refused, apparently using me as an excuse. "My wife would kill me."

One man shot back at him. "Don't worry about what she thinks." And then he used some choice words, which I'd rather not mention, to describe me as a female.

I was not Jay's favorite person at the time, but he has a temper, especially when someone messes with a loved one.

He and this fellow exchanged words, and before Jay knew it, there was a knife at his throat. This stranger who, moments earlier, had been fulfilling his need to party was now threatening to kill him.

Jay, in pure panic, was able to talk himself right out of the house and down the road back to where Savannah, Noah, and I had just finished reading bedtime stories.

Jayson didn't tell me this story until years later, when he explained that this was the moment he knew he had taken the drinking too far. He also said this was the first time since he'd been saved that he'd felt the nudge from the Holy Spirit.

That was when I realized—and I say this tucking in my pride—that Jayson was and is special. God was protecting him as well, in ways we can't fathom. We didn't know it then, but this was all part of God's plan for a godly man to be born out of an impossible situation. God had a plan to use Jayson in a way we could have never imagined.

This would be the start of the change in Jayson.

Chapter Nine

Storm Clouds

The scary incident at the stranger's house affected Jayson, and he had felt the Holy Spirit bring him through that uncomfortable situation, but the alcohol had gotten a hold of him.

I thought it would take a miracle for us to recover from the hurtful words, the fights, and the way he would leave and be replaced by the worst version of himself when he was drinking.

But in July of that year, as the kids and I enjoyed the summer and prepared for the upcoming school year, I needed Jay, and we both began to feel a strong need for God. We still slept in different beds, rarely talked, and would only see each other most days merely in passing. There were times when divorce seemed to be the only remedy. But I didn't even have the strength to take those steps.

My health was becoming a problem due to all the stress and anxiety I had developed. I felt so alone and started experiencing pains and mental fog like I had never known. Then a hard thing happened that would be the beginning of my realizing my desperate need for God and true need for my husband as well.

I noticed a painful spot on my lower spine that I could not keep my hands off of. For weeks, I found myself rubbing or cupping my hands around that area. I lived with an icepack tucked in the top of my pants to help dull the pain and help me function. Day after day, as the pain got worse, my fear increased, and I wondered what was going on.

I'd be in the shower or doing dishes, and intense pain would shoot from the bottom of my spine to the top of my neck, bringing me to my knees. I had never felt pain like this. I was only thirty and had always been healthy. I couldn't be down or out of commission; my kids and all the responsibilities of a mother were waiting for me.

I couldn't ask Jay for help. I wouldn't admit that I needed him. But eventually, my pain got so bad, I had to tell him that I was no longer able to carry Noah, or even stand long enough to do the dishes. I even had to be careful just lying down. The pain was unbearable.

I spent many days that summer lying still on my bed, trying not to move at all so I wouldn't feel that terrible pain. When I got up to shower, I found myself praying in desperation, with tears of pain pouring out.

> He has also set eternity in the human heart.
> Ecclesiastes 3:11 NIV

At this point in my life, I still didn't understand my relationship with God. Even so, I would find myself naturally whispering, "God, please help me."

With tears rolling down my cheeks and pain shooting to my toes and back up to my neck, I became terrified of what it might mean.

I didn't know it then, but this would be the first of many times on my journey of change that I would have to get knocked down so I'd remember to rely on God. This was only the beginning of the biggest series of storms that Jay and I would face together.

I talked to a few friends and family, telling them what was going on with my back. A couple of friends suggested I go to a chiropractor—just typing that word makes me cringe. I decided to follow their advice.

The doctor took an x-ray and told me that my spine was out of place and that he would need to do an adjustment. That sounded easy enough. I knew plenty of people who did that regularly. I decided to let him do the adjustment, thinking it might be an easy fix.

To my dismay, I went home feeling like I had been hit by a truck. I never knew that my insides could hurt as much as they did. I lay there at a definite pain level of ten plus, with chills settling in all over me. I couldn't do anything but lie in bed shaking while my body was in complete shock from whatever was going on. I had no control over this and no idea what had happened or what to do to help it.

I continued to pray, tears never seeming to cease. "God, help me."

This went on for about four weeks before I finally decided I needed to try to do something else.

Thankfully, several months before my back pain began, Jay and I had been playing our normal Thursday night gig at a local bar. We were approached by a couple we had known for years. They'd always been supportive of the Stovers and would show up to many of our gigs. During conversation that evening, Jayson told them he needed to start looking for a better job.

"If you want a job," the man said, "I can get you one."

They talked for a short time, and by the end of that week, Jay had a job that paid more than we had ever made, with very good insurance.

I decided, since we now had insurance, that I would make a doctor's appointment for my back and for an overall checkup. I hadn't been to the doctor in years, other than for my OB appointments with my two pregnancies.

The reality was that Jayson hadn't been feeling well for some time either. I didn't know what was going on with him. I hadn't paid much attention, nor did I have much sympathy for him at that time. But I convinced him that he, too, should go for a checkup.

He'd been feeling some sort of protrusion in his upper abdomen that had been bothering him for months. He was always poking around at it and asking people to feel it. I had said it felt like a blown-up bodily organ.

We both knew deep down that whatever it was, it was not supposed to be there. We also knew that this was uncharted territory for us. Between my pain and his weird lump, something was wrong.

I was so worried about my back, and the fact that I couldn't take care of the kids and the house like I used to, that I had become a big ball of worry again. I felt I couldn't go on living until we got to the bottom of these health issues. Jay and I were still not getting along, and at this time in my life, I felt no sense of security in anything.

We lived in the apartment, still playing music for rent money, because all of Jay's paychecks were going to our debt. Fighting was still our only—exhausting—form of communication. Stress had taken over our life, our marriage was a mess, and now our health was a concern.

One summer evening in 2014, Jay and I finally took time to discuss these new worries. We walked outside, where the kids couldn't hear. Standing under the stars on a beautiful, clear night, we connected with each other for the first time in years. We found we agreed on one thing: we were scared. Something was happening. Something was different. And something was terribly wrong. We didn't know what it was or how to prepare for it, but we both felt it.

I was afraid that my back pain was a big deal and that I would never get better. How could I take care of my children? Would I ever work again or clean the house like I wanted? Could I be the wife that Jay desired me to be?

He was scared too. He'd been spinning his wheels for so long, trying to provide for our family. He's a dreamer; that's just who he is. But dreams don't always turn out the way you want, and his had gotten so twisted over the years. Music worked until it didn't, and it *wasn't* anymore.

And he was worried about his health. He admitted he hadn't felt well for months. He knew something was wrong but didn't know the extent. He pointed out that he'd been losing weight, no matter how much he ate. I had noticed that. There was something foreign growing in his abdomen, and he couldn't deny it any longer.

We were both selfishly fearing for our own health, but also for the health and future of our family. We didn't know what was happening.

Standing there, Jay and I both began to cry, and for the first time in a long time, we drew each other near in a loose hug as the walls began to come down.

Thoughts rushed through my mind. *Am I dying? Is he dying? Are we going to split up? Will this pain ever go away?*

I turned my head to the right to rest it on Jay's shoulder. He

felt like a stranger to me. My touch didn't recognize his smaller, frailer frame. How long had it been since we'd hugged?
Why did he feel so frail?

I opened my eyes a little through the tears and, to my surprise, noticed what looked like an incredible wall of storm
clouds coming right at us. The night was dark, but the wall of
clouds was a mixture of gray and white and appeared to reach
from the ground to the sky. These clouds were so enormous
that I couldn't see where they began or where they ended.
They stretched each way as far as I could see.

It was a terrifying sight. It looked like something out of a
movie, right before a huge storm comes and destroys everything in its path. It nearly took my breath away.

As I urged Jayson to look, I could tell he had already caught
a glimpse of it. Neither of us had words. We could only stand
there in awe at what we were seeing.

Is this real?

As we stood outside on that summer evening, looking at
the wall of clouds, our insides shuddered. We held each other
as tears squeezed out, still gazing at the wall of clouds. We had
no idea what was coming but felt the storm was about to hit.

After a long silence, we walked back inside. There was so much
more that we needed to say, but neither of us had the strength that
night to begin mending years of unspoken apologies.

It never did rain that evening, and I haven't seen anything
like that since.

Sometimes there are seasons when the only thing we can
do in life is the next thing. That was what Jay and I did for
days until we could get in with the doctor.

A week later, we finally went for our new-patient appointments. The doctor did physicals and ordered blood work for
each of us. She examined my back and ordered physical ther-

apy, explaining that I needed time and therapy to heal.

Without giving us details, she noted her concerns about Jayson's problem in his abdomen and ordered some blood work. I'm sure she knew what we were looking at, but she waited on the proof from the blood work to confirm her thoughts.

Our appointments were on a Thursday, and we figured we wouldn't hear anything until that following Monday. I decided I would try to relax that evening, as there was nothing further I could do.

After dinner, I went to get a pedicure and enjoy some time away from the house. As I got comfortable in the pedicure chair in the middle of the mall, soaking away my worry, my phone rang. It was the doctor's office. And it was after hours.

The nurse explained that she had tried calling Jayson's phone but couldn't get hold of him. She informed me that some of his blood work had come back, and the numbers were higher than anything they had ever seen. The nurse emphasized that he needed to get to the ER immediately.

I sat there in disbelief, trying to absorb the news. I'd thought my health issue was the serious one, but it was Jayson's.

I tried to be calm as I informed the gal doing my pedicure that I had an emergency and needed to leave. While she rushed to slap on the paint—acting a bit annoyed with me—I called Jayson to tell him about the call from the nurse. He answered the phone, and I could tell he already knew. He said he had received the message and had spoken to the nurse. He sounded anxious and—as he always does when he's worried—began acting angry.

When the girl finally finished the polish on my toes, I

waddled out of the mall as fast as I could in my flimsy yellow pedicure flip-flops.

Driving home, I began feeling the same feelings I had felt when I received the call about my dad.

What was happening?

I was the one who had been experiencing debilitating pain for weeks. *I* had been nursing this back pain, not even knowing how it had occurred. I'd been so worried that there was some big underlying issue, since there were so many unknowns, but the nurse had confirmed that *my* blood work, at that time, was great.

Years later, I would be diagnosed with spondyloarthropathy, which is an inflammatory autoimmune disease. That diagnosis made the pain I had learned to deal with over time finally make sense.

It was Jayson though. Something was very wrong with Jayson.

I realized at this point how I had been disgusted with him for so long that I hadn't taken the time to even look at him. I mean *really* look at him.

I was still in victim mode.

On my way home, I called my mom to see if she could sit with the kids so I could go to the hospital with Jay. Our relationship with her and Mark had improved immensely since we moved back—the kids even called them Gar and Pop-Pop. They lived just around the corner from us, and she agreed to come get the kids so that I could be with Jay.

When Mom arrived, Jayson and I took off for the hospital. It was one of the quietest rides we have ever taken together. The questions were just too many to even start to voice, and we both knew that. The tension between us prevailed, and this was almost too much to bear.

124

I couldn't help looking at him and then looking away, thinking, *He's so skinny.* Then I started thinking about the huge bruises he'd been showing me, that would appear on his body, and my mind raced. I sucked in my complaints about how badly the bumpy road hurt my back as we both felt the pressure of the storm barreling our way.

The need for answers felt overwhelming, and the shock of the phone call still hadn't fully sunk in.

Why was blood work an emergency?

He didn't look like he was an emergency. He had just been playing his guitar at the house with the kids on that beautiful summer day.

How had I not noticed he was sick?

We didn't have to wait long to hear the diagnosis that would change everything.

Arriving at the hospital, we found the medical staff waiting for us. The doctor had called to tell them that Jayson was on his way. They took us straight to a room. Shortly after, a lab technician came into the room to redo some of the blood work. By this time, neither of us could hold in the questions any longer.

We both began urgently asking, "What is going on? Why is this an emergency?"

Without even looking at us, one of the nurses answered as she moved about the room. "Well, if it looks like a duck and quacks like a duck, it must be a duck."

> Call upon Me in the day of trouble; I will deliver you, and you shall glorify Me.
> Psalm 50:15 NKJV

I was about to explode. We had no idea what she was talking about. No one had even told us what they thought was going on, so we didn't know what "duck" she was referring to.

"What duck?" I asked.

She finally stopped moving and looked at us. "Cancer."

Cancer? The world stopped.

And then, like most people do when they hear the "C" word, we freaked out.

Suddenly, everything became more serious. We sat there silent as the puzzle pieces we had shrugged off for so long came together in our minds.

"What do you mean, cancer?" Jay finally said.

That was when we heard the word *splenomegaly* for the first time. The nurse explained that Jay's lab numbers were so high because his spleen had been filling up with blood. It was to the point where it could rupture. They had never seen numbers as high as his, which was why they wanted to repeat the lab work.

We were educated soon after hearing the diagnosis, learning that splenomegaly is the most common symptom that patients with chronic myeloid leukemia present with as the spleen begins to enlarge and cause discomfort.

Well, that explained why I thought the lump Jayson kept pressing on felt like an organ.

After their brief explanation, they began examining his skin and pointed out the big bruises we had been seeing for so long.

My tears started in that room, and I couldn't turn them off. I don't know if it was from relief that we finally knew what the problem was or fear of what was about to happen. Maybe it was just the culmination of emotion that had been building for years, knowing that something had to give . . . and this was it. Or maybe the combination of everything.

Looking at him in that ER hospital bed, I saw it.

He didn't look good.

Then I felt terrible. I had gotten used to seeing him as

the bad guy. But now I was seeing things in a different light.

How had I not noticed he was dying? What kind of a person was I?

I realized in that hospital room just how much everything in my life had started to pile up. The drinking, the fighting, the debt, and now the growing health issues that we could no longer ignore.

I still hadn't dealt with all that had happened to me in my early life. My mind and body were a mess from years of worry, anxiety, grudges, and unforgiveness. Now I piled on more, regretting the last couple of years of my life with Jayson.

I realized that my victim mentality was not doing anyone any good. It was time for me to come out of that mindset if there would truly be any lasting healing or any real change.

What had we been thinking? We didn't appreciate anything we had and only strived for *more* and *better*.

I couldn't stop the sadness and regret that seeped out of me. My tear-filled eyes were screaming, *I'm done!*

But the biggest shock—and blessing—for me through all of this was that when I heard the diagnosis, I instantly fell back in love with Jayson. It felt like everything bad that had happened evaporated.

It's crazy how seeing a glimpse of your future, like finding out your husband might die soon, can change your course of action.

I didn't want to leave his side. I couldn't stop hugging him and crying for him and caring for him. That quickly, all the anger I'd had toward him was trumped by compassion and love.

We needed each other, and this traumatic event pushed

us closer together and forced us to recognize the love we still shared, admit our need for each other, and realize how much we were going to need to depend on God.

Chapter Ten

Unidentified Mountains

Once the new tests had been run and numbers confirmed, Jay and I were told that he would have to be transferred by ambulance to a bigger hospital about an hour away. They gave me an hour to go home and pack a bag for us to spend the night in the hospital.

I got in my car, took a deep breath, and wiped away the tears. I tried to focus on the road, my mind spinning.

By the time I had made sure the kids were taken care of, gathered our things, and got back to the hospital, the ambulance had arrived. They let me get in the passenger seat while they wheeled Jay out and put him in the back with a paramedic by his side.

The way everyone talked and acted, like he might die on the way to the hospital, I got more scared than I'd already been.

This ride felt so bumpy! My back was in knots from the pain I was dealing with, and I cried the entire way to the hospital. I tried to stop, but I just couldn't. All the emotions that had been building for the past couple of years finally came to a head.

In a way, I felt relieved because I knew something had to give to break the tension cycle between us, but never would I have imagined this would be the circumstance to do that.

So much had happened in the last couple of hours. I felt as though we were in a dream. Then the silence broke.

Laughing, Jayson yelled to the front. "Heather! Are you okay up there?"

I bit my lip and took a deep breath. "Yep, doing good, how about you?" I tried not to let him know I was crying, but he knew. They all knew. I couldn't stop.

Once we finally arrived at the hospital, we were again taken straight to a room where another medical team awaited us. Jay was still on a bed, and I felt pain every time I moved. I learned then and there to deal with the pain better. I was forced to; what Jayson faced was way more serious. I didn't talk about my pain anymore. I tried to keep my attention and everyone else's on Jay.

I asked how long this had been going on. The doctors estimated a year. Jayson had been fighting a serious disease for a year, and we hadn't known.

This meant that ever since we had moved into John's house, Jayson had been dealing with an invisible disease. All the drinking, all the worrying, all the fighting, had been done while he was not feeling right and didn't understand what was going on in his own body.

All the alcohol he'd consumed, which had made me so furious, had been an unconscious attempt to mask his feelings of illness. All the fights had really stemmed from his worry and unease over what was happening in and around his body. He'd been riddled with questions of why he was so tired, why he ate so much and still lost weight, and why he was getting those mysterious bruises on his stomach and upper thighs.

All this finally made sense to both of us.

And though Jayson obviously had faults that caused problems in our marriage, I could see where I had fallen short as well. I had focused my time and energy on the kids because of my own childhood. I was so determined to make sure they had a wonderful childhood full of good memories that I had completely neglected the fact that Jayson needed me to be a wife too. I should have been helping him instead of blaming him like I had blamed my own dad.

My lost love for Jayson was found again in these hospital rooms. I remembered the man I had married, the man who was fun and adventurous. The man who would pick me up on a Friday and drive all night to Nashville to have a fun weekend. The man who had snuck breakfast and flowers through my trailer window and who had planted daisies in my front yard while I was at work. My guitar player, my children's father, my partner to go through life with, the one God had matched me with perfectly.

Now here he was, lying in a hospital bed on an oncology floor, stricken with fear, being poked every few minutes, hooked up to an IV, ingesting medicine every couple of hours, and waiting on a specialist to diagnose his future. I sat quietly looking out the hospital window, drowning in my own tears, and feeling like I was living someone else's life.

As night approached, I decided to go to the restroom and

wash up a little before I went to sleep for the night. I remember being in the bathroom and trying hard not to touch any surfaces. But despite my attempts to be cautious, I was frazzled and tired and dropped my toothbrush in the sink.

I don't know why it was so momentous, but time seemed to stand still. Something hung in the air around me. I was given complete stillness to make my decision. To use the toothbrush or not to use the toothbrush? That was the question.

I decided I wasn't going to worry, and I really wanted to brush my teeth, so I used it.

That night, we were woken up every hour for Jay to be checked and poked with needles holding medications that no one ever explained to us. No one communicated about what was going on, and we didn't ask questions. Doctors and nurses moved quickly in and out as we lay there not saying much at all. We didn't know what to say.

We were eventually told that Jay would need a bone marrow biopsy the next morning, since the testing showed that his cancer was more than likely leukemia. This test would involve his lying on his stomach and the doctor inserting a large needle down into his pelvic bone to draw out fluid, and then a bigger needle going into the bone to rotate and draw out a piece of bone and tissue to biopsy.

Jay decided he didn't want any pain medicine during this procedure.

When he was wheeled down for the test the next morning, I walked behind them until we reached another unit where the biopsy would be done. Jay went in behind a curtain, where I could no longer see what was happening. But shortly after he disappeared behind the curtain, a very large male orderly joined him. This man looked like he had just walked off a football field. He had been called after Jay informed them of his decision not to get the numbing medication.

The procedure was going to hurt, bad. I knew Jay had made this decision to show he wasn't as weak as they were all treating him. But that's Jay. Tell him he can't do something, and he'll do everything he can to prove you wrong. He needed this man for support. I could tell this man felt for Jay and respected his decision. He talked him through it while holding him down with his enormous arms.

Jay felt every bit of his bone being extracted from his body and was quiet when they wheeled him back to the room.

The next day, he asked my mom and stepdad to bring his guitar to the hospital. I will admit to some annoyance at this request because of the grudge I had built against the music itself, but I knew he needed that comfort. He needed the gift God had blessed him with to spark some joy in his soul amid all the worry and fear that threatened to take over his very being.

My mom and Mark dropped the kids off with their great-grandparents and eventually arrived with the guitar. Within an hour of the guitar's presence within those quiet walls, we were released from the hospital. This surprised us, as we had been told we would be there much longer. But we were not going to argue about being discharged.

Jay still jokes that they released him because they thought he was going to be loud playing the guitar with all those sick patients around.

Maybe that was the reason.

A couple of days later, the results were confirmed that the duck was a duck after all. Jay had CML (chronic myeloid leukemia). He was assigned to a nearby oncologist, whom he would have to see regularly.

The doctor advised that he would have to take one chemo pill a day and hope that would clear the disease. Then, with me sitting quietly beside him, Jay came right out and asked how long he had to live. The doctor replied that the medicine he was putting him on had worked for up to ten years in some patients, but it was so new they didn't know beyond that.

He then went on to say, "But you could walk out of my office and get hit by a truck, so I really can't answer your question."

I'm always a fan of humor, but I couldn't stop focusing on the first answer.

Ten years?

That wasn't long.

I told myself to stay strong for Jayson, and I tried hard not to cry, but I couldn't hold it in. Due to my lack of self-control, this was the last appointment I would ever be allowed to attend. Jayson banned me from any more doctor's visits for being too emotional.

The doctor gave us the prescription and told us he would do everything he could to help with the price. Jay informed him that we had pretty good insurance and that it would be okay.

"I don't think you understand the cost of this medicine." The doctor looked at us kindly. "It's over fourteen thousand dollars a month."

He was right! We never dreamed it would be anywhere near that price.

The doctor started giving instructions on taking the medication and mentioned some side effects to look for. This medication was a chemo pill that would control the blood cells that were multiplying at an astronomical rate.

Jay would need to wear a glove when handling the pill and wash his hands after touching it. He needed to take it with plenty of water. And then came the big blow.

There could be no consumption of alcohol while on this medication.

My world stopped at this statement.

Of course, Jay questioned this. "What do you mean, no alcohol? Not even a drink here and there?"

"None." The doctor raised a stern brow. "Or it will alter the way the medicine works, and you could die."

Jay and I were stunned at this statement; me with relief, him with disbelief.

> I know the plans I have for you," declares the Lord, "plans to prosper you and not to harm you, plans to give you hope and a future.
> Jeremiah 29:11 NIV

We went home with a month's supply of the medication and follow-up appointments scheduled.

I couldn't shake what we had just heard. No alcohol meant my husband's entire world would have to change. He'd be home at night. He would no longer have the anger from whiskey in his body. There would be no more bars and no more late-night gigs revolving around alcohol.

I knew in my heart that God had just given us an enormous blessing. Jay had to quit, and we had to stay away from temptations to ensure he did.

There was no alternative—other than death—but I knew this was not going to be an easy road for him.

Jayson and I finally decided that with all that was happening and all the stress we had been dealing with financially, we would need to file for bankruptcy. It's crazy now to think how ashamed we'd felt when we'd talked about bankruptcy before the diagnosis, because after the diagnosis we realized it was a huge blessing. Bankruptcy would free us to be able to afford these medical bills and the medicine. We promptly filed the paperwork and were approved to get rid of all the debt we had so irresponsibly incurred over the past couple of years.

In the first few days of Jayson's being on this new medication, I was stricken with even more fear. The focus on money was gone, and I had to trust that God would take care of that. My focus was only on Jayson's recovery.

He would fall asleep, and I'd force myself to stay awake, making sure he was breathing, just as I had done with my infants. I woke up throughout the night and quietly checked that his chest was still rising and falling. I worried about him day and night. All the worry wore me out, and my own health diminished.

Within days of being home from the hospital, I got sick. I had caught a virus, probably from the hospital (remember the toothbrush?). Then Jay caught whatever it was from me. We were not used to being sick. We had been healthy for so many years.

I talked about going to the doctor, but Jay said he felt like he was getting better, and he was the one with cancer. He said that if he could beat this virus on his own with the way his immune system was, then so could I.

So I waited.

Meanwhile, Jay's anger had done nothing but increase. Between processing the diagnosis and coming off the alcohol, he had become impossible to live with. But I had found a new level of patience within and let everything go.

I had begun living like he was dying.

This was not a good thing for anyone. My tears rarely stopped as stress took over. I started getting terrible headaches and couldn't function without round-the-clock pain relievers. This was something I had never experienced before.

After Jay had been recovered from the virus for weeks, I finally broke down and went to the doctor. She told me I had a severe sinus infection and prescribed an antibiotic. I carried that bottle of antibiotics around with me for days, with too much anxiety to even put those pills in my mouth. I had been taking painkillers like they were candy but had grown fearful of any new medicine. I was afraid of everything. I had developed what they call *neophobia*—extreme or irrational fear or dislike of anything new or unfamiliar.

Fear was yet again taking over my life.

On September 17, 2014, a few weeks after our hospital trip, I was making my way up the stairs after doing laundry in the basement. I realized my eyesight was a bit distorted. I had let this sickness go on for too long, hoping I could beat it on my own. I asked Jay if my eyes looked okay.

At first, he blew me off as he usually did, chalking it all up to my anxiety (can't blame him). But then, he did a double take and walked right up to my face to get a better look. My anxiety increased by the second.

He studied my face for a minute. "Your eyes look fine, but what's wrong with your mouth?"

"My mouth?"

I ran to the mirror and looked very closely at my facial features. The left side of my mouth appeared to be falling, or what we would soon learn is medically called "drooping." My headache pounded harder, my eyesight got blurrier, and the dizziness increased.

Of course, we jumped on Google, which should never be done when you feel something isn't right. But as we searched my symptoms, everything we read pointed to a stroke. Google says the five warning signs of a stroke are sudden weakness on one side of the body, sudden speech difficulty, sudden difficulty seeing in one or both eyes, sudden onset of dizziness, and severe headache with no known cause.

Not wanting to scare the kids, I ran outside and called my doctor while standing in the same place where we had seen the storm clouds roll in just a couple months before.

My doctor took my after-hours phone call. She advised that everything I was explaining sounded like Bell's palsy, but there was a chance it could be a stroke. She told me to go to the emergency room so they could rule out stroke, implying that Bell's palsy was the diagnosis we wanted.

I ran back inside and asked Jay to Google "Bell's palsy." The pictures that popped up were horrifying.

This was what I was *hoping* for?

We learned in a quick search that Bell's palsy is the sudden weakness of one side of the face that causes drooping. The exact cause is unknown, but it is thought to be a side effect from a virus, or from stress.

Hmmmm. I was a prime candidate for this, but neither option was good.

At this point, everyone in my life was so annoyed with my anxiety that they didn't take anything I said seriously. I can't blame them, as I pretty much thought I was dying from an anxiety attack every other Monday. So I gathered my things and drove myself down the road to the same ER we had gone to for Jay's emergency.

In just that twenty-minute drive, the left side of my tongue went completely numb, and there was a pain in my left ear that hadn't been there even when I called the doctor. Upon arrival, I calmly let the receptionist know what was going on. I was taken to a room for an evaluation to rule out stroke. The whole time, my symptoms progressively worsened.

When the ER doc came in, she had me stick out my tongue, lift my eyebrows, make a kissy face, smile, and crinkle my nose. When I could do all these things, she continued to check my vitals and ordered some blood work. She then assured me that I was not having a stroke. This was obviously a relief, until she diagnosed me with Bell's palsy of the left side of the face, just as my doctor had thought.

After hours of waiting on tests to come back and a long discussion with the doctor, they instructed me to take ibuprofen as needed but to be prepared, because this could get worse over the next forty-eight hours. I was advised that I might need to buy an eyepatch because sometimes you can't close the eye on the affected side, as it becomes paralyzed. They also told me I might notice drooling on that side of my mouth and the inability to eat or drink because my mouth would not completely close normally.

They warned me that this could be my new normal for an unknown amount of time going forward.

I called Jay to let him know what had happened and what the final verdict was. I played it cool, since I didn't want to add any more stress to his life, and obviously my diagnosis didn't compare to his.

As I drove home alone in the middle of the night, my anxiety flew off the charts. I knew I had to get hold of my emotions, or I was going to end up going crazy. I had no control over what was happening to my body, and my anxiety was only making it worse. Furthermore, the doctor had said there wasn't much they could do. She'd said they could put me on steroids to try to decrease the swelling in my head, which was causing the Bell's palsy but that, ultimately, I would have to let it run its course.

When I got home, everyone was in bed and the house was dark. I took a shower and crawled into bed, the left side of my mouth feeling as though it was falling to the floor.

I had no control over this. I had no control over Jayson's

disease. If all this could happen over the course of three months, what else could happen in our lives?

I felt helpless.

I lay in bed, feeling the left side of my face continue to swell. The left side of my tongue was completely numb, and my left eye was losing strength in the muscles around it.

My need for God was becoming obvious. I couldn't rely on myself, and the doctors couldn't do anything more for me.

I closed my eyes, thanking God that I could still manage some movement, then resorted to prayer. I finally hit a point of exhaustion where I gave up on my own strength and whispered again to God.

Please make this stop.

The next morning, I walked to the mirror timidly, scared of what I would find. To my surprise, the paralysis had stopped right below my eye. It was only from my cheekbone down, which was where it had been when I'd started praying.

God had heard me.

God had answered my prayer!

That day, God became more real to me than ever, and I felt grateful. I was reassured that He was the only one who could really help me. Even more, I was learning that God was the only one in control at all.

Jay and I both would learn a huge lesson in this season. God was pushing us just far enough to realize we would need to rely on Him and no one else. We were learning to pray and trust. Learning to run to God, our Father, in prayer and rest in Him for comfort.

At this point, all we knew was that Jayson had to stop drinking, we had to keep praying, and we had to trust that this was all part of God's plan for our life. All we could do was keep getting up, pushing through life together, and enjoying the good days. The days when we could go out and enjoy the sunshine together. The days like all the others before, when we hadn't recognized we were resting on the mountain.

Our good days now were when Jay came home from the doctor and said that his labs were looking better and that the medication was working.

After months of dealing with the Bell's palsy, I recovered from the swelling and droopiness. But I have never fully recovered from that illness. Even today, eight years after my diagnosis, my tongue still goes numb, and my face still droops when I let worry bog me down. When I allow anxiety to take over my body, my face feels as though it is sliced down the middle, and that whole side throbs in pain as the memories from the illness creep back in.

I truly feel like this has been God's way of teaching me not to let the worry go too far, because I am not in control, and I need to give my worries over to Him. When my face starts hurting and numbness sets in, I am reminded that it's time to pray more, take deep breaths, and remove the weight from my shoulders and offer it back to God.

PART THREE

Looking Forward

"Unless you people see signs and wonders,
you will by no means believe."
John 4:48 NKJV

Chapter Eleven

Turning North

We decided to move again in October 2014. An opportunity for a single-family house came our way, this time a rental property that was just minutes away from the triplex. It was bittersweet leaving John's house. We loved the apartment itself, but we had too many hard and scary memories there. We were ready for another change.

I shared what was happening in our lives with the principal at Savannah's school and asked for prayer. To our surprise, the school offered to adopt our family for Christmas. This was a big step for me. We hesitated to let anyone know how badly we were struggling, but we agreed, and for the first time ever, we let strangers into our lives. Instead of being embarrassed or prideful, we allowed them to bless us. I was learning that this is what Christians do.

The week before Christmas, we received a wealth of gift cards that the school had collected from staff members and parents. Because of their generosity, we were able to give our children a Christmas that otherwise would not have happened. This act of kindness sealed the deal for Jayson and me that these people were our family and that they cared about us, maybe even loved us.

I was growing to love what this school had to offer my children. Savannah was learning scripture, singing praise songs, and learning principles and rules that aligned with biblical teaching. All this from attending only a couple of days a month. We were so impressed with all she was learning and how happy she was that we decided to send her full time the upcoming school year, for second grade.

The truth was, Jay and I were learning right alongside Savannah. We had taken a lot of hits that year, but they had pushed us toward God instead of away. We were thankful for all He had gotten us through and hungry to learn more about Him and His Word. We recognized the fact that our marriage had been healing because of God. We realized we had too many problems to do that in our own strength. The leukemia and Jay's medication had forced him to quit drinking, which had been the very thing that saved our marriage and was leading us both closer to Jesus.

The illnesses had actually been gifts.

> Then the Lord said to me, "You have made your way around this hill country long enough; now turn north."
> Deuteronomy 2:2–3 NIV

God was still doing a work in us though, and it didn't appear He would be easing up soon.

By the summer of 2015, we had settled into the new house and had adjusted to the new challenges we were dealing with. I set up an appointment with a dermatologist for something I had been putting off. I had noticed an unusual growth on my left shoulder about the time we moved back from Florida. I was hoping it would just go away, but no matter what I did to it, it kept coming back bigger and more painful each time.

Jayson was working that day, so I dropped the kids off at Mamaw's house and went to the appointment alone, not knowing what to expect. It only took a glance for the dermatologist to decide that it needed to come off immediately and go for biopsy.

I didn't hear anything for a couple of weeks. My fear of what they would find became a dark shadow between me and God. Once I realized my arm was healed up but I still hadn't heard anything, anxiety took over.

A spot on my body, just a bit larger than a pencil eraser, had me fearing death like nothing I had ever felt before. I had let that tiny little bump steal my joy and my desire to rest in God's plans.

Finally, with the kids at a playdate and Jayson at work, I called the doctor's office. In my mind, life again couldn't go on until I had the assurance that I was okay.

When the nurse answered the phone, I told her my name and why I was calling, feeling like I was annoying her with every word out of my mouth.

"Oh, yes. We received the results." Her tone seemed cheerful. "It was cancer. But we got it."

"Oh, great." I played it off cool, trying to match her demeanor. "Thanks so much."

But when I hung up and the conversation sank in, I panicked.

What? Oh, yes! It was *cancer*.

That word. How it scared me. In my little mind, it equaled death. That was really all I heard. The "C" word. That was all the enemy wanted me to hear. I was learning that Satan doesn't only dwell in hell, where I had always kept him.

> Be alert and of sober mind. Your enemy the devil prowls around like a roaring lion looking for someone to devour.
> 1 Peter 5:8 NIV

Satan was doing his best to hinder my growing relationship with God and His Son, Jesus, whom I had been learning was my true Savior. Satan was sabotaging my mind, and I felt I had no control over this attack.

I began to cry as I got off the phone. Not a happy cry, because the nurse had said that they got it and it was gone. No, I cried the cry of *poor me*, because of that "C" word.

I got in my car, riddled with anxiety, my body full of fear. But this time, I drove to the church that we had been attending.

I was learning where to run.

I walked into the empty sanctuary and sat in the front pew. I never sat in the front pew. At first, I just sat there, looking around. Finally, I bowed my head and attempted to pray, something I still didn't do much of unless I was in desperate pain.

I whispered, "God, I'm scared. What do I do with this?"

God spoke to me in the internal voice that I was beginning to recognize and learning to love and trust. This voice was different from the voice I'd heard as a child. I didn't want to drown out or mask this new voice. I wanted more.

Almost instantly, so tenderly and appropriately, God taught me right there.

Dear, this is not a prayer circumstance, this is a praise circumstance.

Isn't it funny how God works? Every Sunday at that church, we had a time of prayers and praises, where church members passed the microphone around and shared blessings with praise or worries as they asked for prayer. God used that familiar method to ease my mind in seconds.

It was cancer, He said, *but it's gone. Now you praise, and I forgive you for not praying about this, but remember.*

God was teaching me, little by little, that He is in control, that He is worthy of praise, and that when I am fearful or anxiety ridden, I need to go to Him first in prayer. Even in the smallest pencil-eraser-size circumstances.

That experience is something I don't take for granted. The scar on my left arm reminds me even today how He used it to get through to me, in the most sensitive of ways. I knew that we'd have more struggles, more times of fear, more insensitive medical staff, but I knew now that I could trust God. He was teaching me where to go to find peace in everything. He gave me a visual aid, chiseled in my flesh just inches above my heart so I would never forget how close God is and how much He cares for me.

The 2015–2016 school year rolled around that fall, and Savannah started second grade full time at the Christian school our hearts were set on. This was another huge year for us, as we saw change coming more quickly than ever.

One day, I dropped Savannah off at school, then pulled over in the parking lot to allow Noah to sleep in the back seat. I sipped coffee and read the newsletter that the school had sent out that week. A notice seemed to jump off the page. The school needed substitute teachers, and the requirements were a bachelor's degree and, of course, that you were saved and identified as a Christian.

I felt a sudden urge to go into the school and talk to the

principal about this opportunity. I had a bachelor's degree, I believed in God, and I had been saved. My past still made me feel like a fraud at times, but I was learning to be a Christian.

I decided to go for it. I called from the parking lot and told the principal I was interested. She was thrilled and said something to me that I had never heard before.

"You are an answer to prayer."

Me, the girl who had grown up abused, beaten down, and drug addicted? The girl who had sung in bars for years, who had just been told she'd had cancer and whose husband *still* had cancer? The girl who'd just filed for bankruptcy?

Yes. Me, the girl who had no self-confidence and still felt unworthy. I was an answer to prayer.

After a brief conversation and some guidance on how to apply for a substitute license through our state, I landed a job I had never imagined I would even try for.

I was going to work at a Christian school.

Only a day passed before my phone rang for me to come in and sub at this school for the first time. I was nervous. I didn't know how to be a teacher, and I didn't know as much about God and the Bible as most of these children did. But Mamaw and Jay's grandparents were on board to watch Noah, and I was ready for something different. This felt so right.

I went in that day and supervised those children as if they were my own. I heard them reciting scripture and saw them worshipping. I wept that day from the sheer beauty God had allowed me to see. The beauty that this type of lifestyle existed and that there were many, many families who knew how to live as Christians lived.

The more I got called to sub, the more I learned. I walked down the hallways, learning the fruits of the Spirit for the first time as I read the banners lining the hallway. "Love, joy, peace, patience, kindness, goodness, faithfulness, gentleness, and self-control" hung large above my head as I walked from room to room. I said them silently with each step.

I was overwhelmed by these new people and new surroundings that God had led me to, but I had to be careful that they didn't catch on to me. I had to start learning at a quicker pace to keep up with even the children. There were so many times I would dart into the bathroom to break down in tears at the worship I heard and the scripture being recited, and because of the beautiful caring souls surrounding me.

I had never seen anything like this.

Meanwhile, a man at the church we'd been attending had been trying to convince Jayson for some time to go on a spiritual retreat to grow a deeper relationship with Jesus. This was a three-day retreat program that offered separate sessions at different times for men and for women. I had wanted to attend this retreat myself for a couple of years. The thought of spending three days doing nothing but learning about God sounded so refreshing to me.

That March, when Jay finally agreed to go, I was elated, not only for him but because I knew my turn was coming.

When Jayson returned from his three-day retreat, it only took one glance for me to see that something had changed. He had a look of peace and a newfound gentleness, as if he had finally released the feeling of defeat that he'd been clinging to for so long.

After a short reunion at the house, Jay and I tucked the kids into bed and met at the dining room table to talk about his experience. He explained that at first, he'd felt disconnected and unlike the other men at the retreat. He kept his emotions and his fears about his recent diagnosis a secret, not welcoming any pity from anyone. But eventually, throughout those three days, his heart had softened.

He told me, with tears in his eyes, that on the last night of the retreat, he finally felt he had surrendered to God. He found himself literally facedown at the huge wooden cross in the dining hall of the retreat center. Recognizing that God knew everything he was going through, he had found comfort for the first time since his diagnosis.

He heard the Lord speak to him in his heart, saying, *There's a lot of work to do.*

This assured him that he was accepted despite his flaws and mistakes. He felt that God was counting on him for something.

Jayson had always said he'd been saved as a child, but it was during this retreat that he felt *true salvation.*

He said, "Heather, this didn't have anything to do with a preacher or any other man. This was between Jesus and me."

Jayson had come back different. Taking the time to sit at the feet of our heavenly Father had made him act and even appear more like Jesus. This was huge. He was experiencing change, but I felt it through him as well.

The weeks that followed would only prove more and more that God is faithful and that what He says is true.

Jayson went to his next routine doctor visit two weeks after his time with Jesus. He sat in the office on a beautiful spring day, waiting to hear the results of his blood work. The doctor slowly opened the door. As she entered the room, she smiled and asked Jayson to stand up, then embraced him.

"I very rarely get to say this to anyone," she said, "but looking at your latest lab results, I see no trace of any leukemia in your body!"

Unable to hold back the tears, Jayson instantly remembered God and praised Him in that moment. Looking at the doctor, he said, "I recently had a blood transfusion."

Her puzzled look requested more explanation.

"I now have the blood of Jesus running through my body," he explained. "I have been cleansed."

As Jayson left that office, he realized he had been truly born again and given another chance. He knew that for the rest of his life, God deserved his praise and to be glorified for what He had done in him and for him.

By April of that year, it was my turn to attend the retreat. I couldn't wait, especially after seeing the change that Jayson had gone through in the short time since he had been back.

When I arrived at the retreat, we were all referred to as "pilgrims." The first thing on the agenda was to have an extended time of silence. I welcomed every second of that time. My life had seemed so loud for so long. As I sat there, silent and alone, I suddenly remembered the maddening echo I had heard as a child whenever the silence would come.

I thanked God in my silent prayers for taking that away. I then thanked Him for the improvement I had seen in my life since meeting Jayson. Even though our years together had been rocky, they had been far better than my childhood.

When the silent time was over, we listened to a few speakers. We were then assigned to a table with the women who would be our group for the remainder of the retreat. There we had group discussions. We worshipped together, took communion, and prayed for one another. The songs we sang were all new to me, but singing them helped me focus on Jesus.

Music—or more accurately, my past with music—had become an embarrassment to me, and I would feel ashamed if anyone happened to mention it. But on day two, I grabbed a tambourine for the first time since doing the bar shows. Being in this atmosphere, singing these songs of praise—my heart was learning to sing again.

That evening, we were encouraged to pray about something we wished we could let go of. Something that stood in the way of our relationship with Jesus. As I asked God which thing I should let go of, He put one word in my head that I couldn't get away from: *Worry.*

His tender voice spoke simply. *Give Me your worry, child.*

He acknowledged me as His child that day, and I accepted Him as my only true Father.

I broke down as I felt chains breaking all around my body at this realization. Little by little, God stripped me of all the things that held me back from a true, lasting relationship with Him. He had already begun stripping any feelings of the control I thought I had. He had been stripping fear, and now He was stripping worry from my life.

> Cast all your anxiety on him because he cares for you.
> 1 Peter 5:7 NIV

I was learning that only He knew what should go. As He stripped those things away, all that was left was what was meaningful.

I learned about God and more about His Son, Jesus. I learned that Jesus is always with me and wants me to let Him carry my load of problems and anxieties. I learned that Jesus died on the cross to take my sin and that since He had taken it, I didn't have to carry it anymore. I learned that God didn't stay in the sky where I had always imagined Him but that He lived inside my body, in the Spirit that I had received. I learned that He wanted me to let Him take the burdens I'd held on to for so long.

I came back from the retreat feeling like a brand-new person. I wanted to be around people more. I wanted to talk about God. I wanted to praise Him for all He had done in my life. My chains were being broken one by one as I handed over my worry and anxiety to Jesus.

He was changing me to mirror the image of God, just as He had intended in creation.

When the next school year rolled around, Noah started pre-K at the school Savannah still attended. They asked me to come onboard as a part-time staff member, monitoring elementary recess and high school study hall. The schedule worked out great, aligning with the time my children would be there. I felt so blessed to be able to be with them and to keep learning from other families and staff members who were so deeply rooted in Christ.

In the 2017–2018 school year, Savannah was in fourth grade, and Noah started full-time kindergarten. I decided that since both kids would be in school all day, I would apply for a full-time position in the office, where I could use my business degree.

I met with the superintendent for an interview and, to my surprise, spent more time talking about my testimony—a required part of the application process—than anything else. He told me that he was drawn in, reading my testimony and how God had caught me off guard that stormy night in 2010. We spoke briefly about my childhood, me only sharing the answers to his questions and the fact that I didn't grow up in a Christian home. I, of course, left the ugliness out of that conversation.

Before our meeting ended, he said something that would stick with me, just as the principal had back in my first job interview.

"You know, Heather," he said, "I gather that you and your husband are a first-generation Christian family. You are making lasting changes that will affect your family for generations to come. Don't forget that."

I had never thought of it that way. I still felt like somewhat of a fraud, because I was holding on to the lie that I was undeserving and unworthy to live a good life. But he made it clear that he saw right through me and that it was okay. He encouraged me to keep going with this lifestyle Jayson and I were diving into.

I didn't get the job that I interviewed for that day. Instead, I was called into the elementary office and offered a job as the full-time preschool aide. I was disappointed at first, but I quickly learned just how amazing God can be when we are obedient to His will.

I accepted the job, and God plopped me right down in preschool to start fresh and learn the stories that the youngest children were learning. Stories that I had never heard. He placed me with one of the best mentors a person could ever ask for. I was to be a teacher's aide for a woman who had attended this school from kindergarten through her senior year and then taught there, right out of college and, at that point, going on thirty years.

This lady was by far the most patient, kind, loving person I had ever known. Everything she said and taught these young children was done from a biblical point of view. I witnessed three-, four-, and five-year-old children learning scripture, being moved to lift their arms in praise, and praying for one another.

She didn't know it, but as she taught the class, she was teaching me too.

Jay was asked to go on the retreat again that year, where he would no longer be a pilgrim but would serve as music leader. They had caught wind that he was an excellent guitar player, and since he had already been a pilgrim, he had all the qualifications. Jay resisted—he didn't play worship music—but I encouraged him to go back, knowing his skill was so profound he could learn a song in minutes.

This retreat, that atmosphere, and those songs would take some time and a different frame of mind to accept. But we both knew this felt right.

Just like on his first time around, Jayson felt disconnected, and he questioned why God had wanted him to go back.

But when another man on the staff approached Jayson and asked, "Do you think you're tough?" Jay realized he didn't appear very humble to others.

This man must have read Jayson's body language and noticed that Jay was not experienced in this type of environment, especially in a leadership position.

Jayson had no response.

Then the man said, "Jesus is tough! If you want to be a man, be like Jesus. He's a true man."

Jayson, obviously taken aback by the statement, couldn't argue the fact or say anything in response to this guy.

The last night of the retreat, exactly one year after the night Jayson felt true salvation, he found himself at that very same cross. This time though, that man walked up and joined him in prayer. He prayed first for Jay and our family, and then, out of nowhere, he prayed for Jayson to be a lead worshipper at a church where they would serve together.

Jayson said he couldn't help but raise an eyebrow as this man continued praying, thinking, *What is he talking about?*

After the prayer, Jayson asked him where he preached.

"I'm not a preacher," the man replied. "I'm a FedEx driver." He offered his hand. "Name's Kenny."

After wrapping up the conversation, Jayson walked away, confused. But the Lord had a plan.

Jayson laughed as he told me this story, explaining that this man was saying they should start a church where the FedEx driver would be the preacher and the construction worker would be the lead worshipper.

The two kept in contact after that retreat. The FedEx driver, whom we would all come to know and love, would eventually become our pastor.

Kenny and his wife, Kim, who are now two of our dearest friends, started holding church in their home in May 2017. Eventually, they purchased a building and held the first official service there on February 11, 2018. Jayson was on the platform leading worship for that service at the new country church, which had been named Olive Tree Christian Fellowship.

We had been feeling like it was time to leave the church we were attending, and no matter how much we resisted, God's will would be done. I agreed to go to the first service at the new church with Jayson but told him I wasn't going to sing. I was just going to feel things out.

We had never led worship. I was so nervous for Jayson!

But sitting in the pew in the new church, with Jayson on the platform leading worship, felt right. Listening to the message, I was moved to tears. Kenny had passion and energy and spoke the truth. His preaching filled me to the top. Our Bibles were open, he pointed us to scripture, and he was real with the congregation, admitting his own flaws and reminding us of ours as well; something I had never witnessed in church.

I was ready to get up there and sing the next service with Jayson and couldn't wait for the next time we could enter those doors.

But this meant that Jayson and I would have to learn worship songs. We had a library of songs we could sing and play, but nothing appropriate for Sunday-morning worship. We felt yet again that God had led us right where we needed to be, and I felt a change like I had never felt before growing in my heart.

It would require time and effort to learn these songs, but we were ready, and music was coming back into our life and our relationship.

Chapter Twelve

Power

Eight years after the initial feelings of God's pursuit, I felt His true power within me, around me, and before me for the first time.

We were finally starting to look like and be the family I had always dreamed of. We bought a house of our own and even got a dog we named Evie Blue. Jay and I were playing music together again—in church—and enjoying it! We were becoming worshippers and leaders. We were familiar with the drill of learning songs and singing them in front of people. We had done that for years. But when we began to learn Christian songs—or what we know now as worship songs—something inside both of us began to change.

That crazy idea of singing in church—the idea that I knew could have only come from God—was coming to fruition. People were paying attention, but not to us; they were there because of their love for God and their desire to worship. This was a whole new ball game. We were no longer trying to gain attention and praise for ourselves. God had given us the opportunity to use our gifts to lead others in worship, and He was now our focus. We were giving *all glory to God* because He is all-deserving, and we had been through enough to know that. We were learning that we could use worship to battle against spiritual warfare and that being obedient to the Word is an offering to God.

The Stovers were now officially the "church group." It was not a gift to take lightly.

> I will sing of Your power; yes, I will sing aloud of Your mercy in the morning; for You have been my defense and refuge in the day of my trouble.
> Psalm 59:16 NKJV

By this time, Jay and I had been on our road to change, drawing near to God, reading God's Word, and studying for a while. But I was about to find out that reading and studying about God are very different from truly knowing and feeling God's presence.

Jayson and I were getting more comfortable leading worship, but we were also beginning to feel God's power within and around us. Our understanding of God was becoming clearer, and our love for Jesus grew beyond anything we had anticipated. For the first time in our lives, it sank in what God had done for us by sending His Son, Jesus, and it didn't make sense not to live for Him and praise Him for the gift of salvation. We recognized that God had been protecting us throughout our lives, even when we were making bad decisions and when bad things were happening around us. We understood that He had been patient with us. But now that we knew the truth, we had a responsibility.

Those health diagnoses were scary and hard, but God had used them to turn us around and get us moving a little further north, the direction we should have turned when we were saved. We had the *title* of worship leaders, but we were *becoming* lead worshippers.

As we drew nearer to God, I noticed that when I sang these songs, something happened to my body. I would be in the shower—the one place I can be alone to pray and sing and be with God—singing songs that we were learning for the Sunday service, and I'd feel an urge to lift my arms. I had seen people lift their arms when they were in church on TV, but I had never attended a church where people actually did this.

There were multiple times when I resisted allowing my arms to do whatever it was they were trying to do. And then one day, my emotions took over. Before I knew it, my arms were raised in the air, and I was weeping.

I didn't understand what was going on, but whatever it was, it felt good.

I had started experiencing this in my private shower time, completely vulnerable yet so comfortable in the confines of my own small bathroom. Then I started to feel these feelings at church during worship. That was uncomfortable.

I don't like to admit this, knowing what I know now, but I was afraid to show any emotion toward

> Praise the Lord, all you servants of the Lord who minister by night in the house of the Lord. Lift up your hands in the sanctuary and praise the Lord.
> Psalm 134:1–2 NIV

God in church. That sounds awful. But this was totally new to me. I didn't understand what was happening to my arms, and I surely was not ready for what was about to happen to my heart. The urge that my arms had to move up started happening every time I sang.

At one point, one arm made it up to about waist level before something inside me pressed it back down to my thigh. It felt like a load of bricks was holding me down. I wish I could say I let go and worshipped with my hands raised high, like I later found commanded many times in the Bible. But I was ignorant about this. My eyes were not fully open to what I had been reading and what I had heard being preached. I was simply going through the motions and trying hard to understand what I was supposed to do with the life I had been given and this newfound relationship between God and me.

One Sunday morning in January 2019, after experiencing these feelings in the shower and on the church platform, the worship felt different. There was something happening in the room. Something supernatural.

When God presents Himself, you just know.

I felt the urge coming on, and I finally broke through the force holding my arms down. I raised my left arm straight to heaven. I was holding the microphone with my right hand, left arm raised, hand pointing north. As soon as this happened, something inside my body began to shake, and then I got dizzy. The room was going in circles, and I had a hard time standing on my feet. I sank to the floor in an effort to regain control over my body. I was instantly exhausted and felt as though I was going to be sick.

> I will praise you as long as I live, and in your name I will lift up my hands
> Psalm 63:4 NIV

We were at the end of the song, so I assumed others just thought maybe I was praying. But really, I was in shock. I didn't know what had just happened. My body felt weightless and empty, like I had literally expelled heaviness.

Looking back, I see that this was the moment that I fully surrendered my life in obedience. I finally broke through the bricks that morning, the bricks that I believe Satan would love to hold over my freedom to worship God. The feelings of apprehension to worship freely and the thoughts of what others would think or say about me vanished after this experience.

I thank God for giving me the strength in that moment to fully surrender, because I had never felt closer to the Father, Son, and Holy Spirit than when I had my arms raised, and eyes closed in worship.

I had finally fully surrendered, and I felt *transformed*.

God had given me the strength to put aside my pride and give myself fully to Him in worship, the way He intended. God had been working on me for years to gain an understanding of Him, to learn to rely on Him, and to remember He was there.

> Submit
> yourselves,
> then, to God.
> Resist the devil,
> and he will flee
> from you.
> James 4:7 NIV

I know this without a doubt, because ever since that day, my worship has *changed*. Ever since that day when I felt those supernatural feelings take over, I have felt free with my worship. Nothing holds me back, and my hands automatically go up when I'm praising the Lord. I know He deserves all of me.

I know without a doubt that the Holy Spirit lives within me and that Jesus is always beside me. God is always watching out for me.

Chapter Thirteen

The Writing on the Wall

It was February 2019, and our lives were busy. I was still working full time at the Christian school our children attended, and Jayson was working more than full-time hours again. The kids and I would leave the school exhausted and rush to appointments or the grocery store, completely missing daylight. When we got home, it was a rush to get homework, dinner, showers, and housework done, only to do it all again the next day.

I thought it was also a good idea to throw a workout into my already busy schedule, because the fast food we were consuming, due to our busyness, was making me feel and look horrible.

But my life felt better than it ever had. Jay and I had built a strong marriage through our trials, and we were all healthy. Jayson still had to take daily medication, but the doctors continued to tell him that his numbers were great and that they saw no trace of the disease in his blood. The only reason he had to stay on the medication was because they didn't know enough about what would happen if he got off.

Jayson had changed because of the disease and had even begun to give public testimony that he believed God had literally cleansed his blood, as Jesus paved the way for him to grow in his faith and newfound Christian life.

God was still teaching us, and it seemed the more obedient we were, the further He took us. But I couldn't have prepared for the next lesson, the next health scare that would impact me even more and make God appear close enough to touch.

On February 13, the kids and I went about our evening as usual. At about seven thirty, they were in their rooms doing homework, and I knew Jay would be home soon. I hurried to finish up my housework so I could do my workout video.

I picked up pillows, folded blankets, and collected dog toys that were scattered around the house. I bent over to pick up a ball from below our flatscreen TV that was mounted on the wall above the fireplace. But then, as I stood up, I crushed my left temple into the corner of the TV. By this time, both the kids were out of their rooms getting a snack and witnessed me fall.

The blow was so forceful, it knocked me right back down on the floor. As I stood up, wincing in pain, I didn't know whether to laugh or cry. So I just laughed it off, not wanting to worry the kids.

There was no time to think about the injury. I thought, *You're an adult, Heather. Move on.* I continued my cleaning and then started the workout, but I could feel the bump growing.

For the next thirty minutes, I did jumping jacks, burpees, and other cardio movements. My vision was a bit distorted, but the pain began to feel more like a throbbing headache than a bump, so I discarded the notion that something could be seriously wrong. I knew how my anxiety worked, and I wasn't going to let it worry me.

I did decide, after I finished the workout, to put some ice on my head, as the bump had grown quite large. Feeling foolish, I applied the ice for what seemed like an adequate amount of time and then took a shower.

When Jay got home from work, I told him what had happened, adding, "If I don't wake up in the morning, you'll know why."

Though outwardly joking, I was serious. The feeling in my head was odd and began to scare me. I prayed God would let me be okay.

That was one of the strangest nights I've ever had. I had become a great sleeper after having children. I often joked that I needed infant sleep, or I wouldn't be on my A game. This night, though, was different. I kept waking with twitches in my head and body. I fell in and out of sleep, waking each time with a headache and dizziness.

When my alarm clock rang, I decided to just go about my busy morning as usual. I didn't know what was going on or what I could do about it. I drove to school with the kids, trying not to overreact. As I walked through the doors of the school, however, I knew something was wrong. My vision was bending, and the lights were glaring. My head still hurt, and the bump on my temple had become very large and tender.

As the morning went on and nausea set in along with my other symptoms, it occurred to me that the head bump might have been worse than I thought.

I called Jayson and explained what I was feeling and that I thought I should go to the ER. He was on a construction job an hour away from the school. I told him I would be fine going by myself and just asked him to leave early enough to pick up the kids from school. I knew ER visits were usually lengthy, no matter the reason for going. Then, even though some caring individuals at the school offered to take me, I again drove myself.

After a fifteen-minute squinty-eyed, shaky drive, I was in the ER. A physician looked at my pupils, assessed my symptoms, and ordered a CAT scan of my brain.

Despite my best efforts, the fear settled in.

I tried to rest while I waited to be taken for the CAT scan, but my head hurt so bad I could hardly stay still. I thought about the people I could potentially call to come in and sit with me. But I didn't want to be a burden to anyone.

Then, as the anxiety and worry crept in, *I remembered Jesus*. The things I had been learning were being put into action, and I remembered that I didn't need anyone else to be with me. I had Jesus living within me, and *He is enough*. I began to pray, asking for help yet again but being comforted instantly at the thought of Jesus holding my hand.

When the CAT scan was over, I was wheeled back to the exam room to wait on the results, feeling a peace that I can only credit to God for allowing His Son to comfort me in my time of trouble.

When the doctor came back in, he let me know that I did indeed have a TBI (traumatic brain injury). I couldn't believe it. I had always thought this was something that happened to football players and people involved in serious auto accidents, not someone who bumps their head on the TV.

The doctor explained that because I had hit my head at

the left temple, it had caused a bruise on my brain. He advised that I get lots of rest and take over-the-counter medication for the headaches. He also said I should stay off all screens and not attempt to read.

So the remedy was to stop life and go lie in my bed, with no internet, cable, or even books.

Then he informed me, just as the doctors had when they diagnosed my Bell's palsy, to be prepared because this would probably get worse.

His exact words were "Some TBIs can get really nasty."

I thought, *Okay, I'll just slow down my life for a bit and take some ibuprofen.*

But I could not have prepared for what was coming.

I was advised that driving was not a good idea, which I knew. I guess I just needed someone to tell me. I let Jayson know so he could ask Mark to come get my car when I was discharged.

When I was finally released, I walked outside to wait for Jay, Mark, and the kids. I leaned against the cold cement wall to steady myself. As they pulled up, I could see the looks of concern on their faces. I tried my best to act normal. I handed Mark the keys to my car and got in Jay's car with the kids. We went home and ate dinner as usual, not knowing that would be the last time I would be able to eat with my family at the table for weeks.

I stayed home from work for the next couple of days and rested on the couch, thinking I would be ready to get back to my life after a good long weekend. Jayson, my mom, and Mark helped with transporting the kids to and from school, since I couldn't drive.

The more I slept, the worse the fatigue seemed to get, and the headaches caused me to take medication around the clock.

The nausea and vision distortion kept me down, as I couldn't bear to keep my eyes open for long.

After a couple of days, my head pounded in pain so bad I couldn't even think straight.

Monday came, but I was not at all ready to get back to my normal life. I was getting worse and was stuck in a dark room by myself, sleeping all day.

I had a follow-up appointment with my family doctor the next week. She advised that my eyes still didn't look good and, since I still had the bad headache, I should continue to rest and come back in another week.

I wanted them to fix this. Why couldn't they give me something to make this go away?

Apparently, Jayson was thinking the same thing, only he wanted *me* to make it go away.

When the next weekend came and I was still in bed, he got frustrated. He came into the room and said, "Heather, you are going to have to get up."

"I want to." I began crying. "But my head hurts so bad, I can't."

Then he sternly argued. "I know how you get, Heather. The depression is going to sink in, and you're going to make this worse on yourself."

I was so hurt that he thought I could do something about this, and I felt so alone. But my history of worry, anxiety, and depression caused his reasonable accusations.

After two weeks of sleeping all but three or four hours a day, I was still hurting and sick and now growing depressed, just as Jayson was afraid I would.

When the depression and fear took over, Satan made it clear that he was taking advantage of this illness and had decided to join me in that room.

One day, as I lay there in the dark, I felt as though Satan were lying beside me and whispering lies in my ear. He said things like "Your kids are fine without you" and "Look, you're not that important. You have been easily replaced in all areas of your life."

Which, technically, I had been. They had found someone to fill in at the school for me. My kids had my mom and step-dad taking them to and from school, and Jayson had stepped up to do the things around the house that I had always done.

Although I should have seen that as a blessing, it hurt and made me feel unneeded and unloved. Satan would haunt my sleep with nightmares, and I got to a point where he felt so present that I literally felt I could see the presence lying beside me, smiling as I suffered in the dark.

I was sinking until finally, I remembered the gift that God had given me.

I had sung the songs about worshipping through the pain or even in the sadness over and over at church. I was convicted that although I had sung those songs as a leader, I was not living them out now that I was facing another trial.

In that moment, I realized my gift from God hadn't been a good singing voice, as others would tell me. My gift was the *ability* to worship.

It was time to live out what I had been preaching.

I began to pray harder and more often.

I prayed for healing, strength, and bravery. I had come too far in my walk with the Lord to let this get me and to sink back onto my easy road of self-pity. I knew the truth, and I began to order Satan out of my bedroom with prayers and praises to God as I lay there. My head hurt so bad most of the time that I would curl my pillow around my temples and squeeze to alleviate the pounding, but I knew what I had to do spiritually. I had learned we are commanded to praise God and that this had been an easy thing to do when life was good, when I was feeling good.

But as I lay there facing a struggle and illness that I didn't understand, my initial reaction had not been to praise. I knew in my heart it would be foolish not to draw closer to God during this time.

I needed Him.

I remembered what the Lord said in His Word: "In this world you will have trouble. But take heart! I have overcome the world" (John 16:33).

He also promised in this passage that in Him we can have peace. There was nothing any other human could do to help me get better. I wasn't allowed to read, text, or even watch TV to try to find comfort elsewhere. I couldn't see to read anything anyway.

But as I was losing physical strength, I was gaining strength spiritually.

I had to stay strong and obey what I had read in the Bible, no matter how I felt or what was happening. So when I was awake, I would pray. I could see my phone enough to push *play* on my worship music, and when everyone else was at work and school, I began to worship instead of allowing communication with Satan. I would sing and lift my hands and cry and pray over and over for strength, healing, and bravery. I had a family and a life to get back to, and I had a direct mission from God along with a spiritual gift to use for His glory. I couldn't let this get me.

It finally became clear to Jayson that this was real, and he started to try harder to take care of me and of things at home. He let others know the severity of what was going on. He told them how I was now absent from life other than my breathing body lying in that dark room.

During my second follow-up appointment with my doctor, she diagnosed me with post-concussion syndrome. Apparently, a TBI can also turn into a concussion, which was my case. I learned that post-concussion syndrome was just another way to say that the symptoms were hanging on longer than expected and were more severe than normal. Research says that this may be due to structural damage to the brain, disruption of the messaging system, or because the emotional reactions to these effects are similar to depression. While this sounded reasonable, I would soon find out that even though the explanation may be common with scientific definitions, God was working a *miracle* and a story in these few weeks that He would use to glorify Himself.

Church members started calling and checking on me. They began praying and sending cards and words of encouragement. They reminded me of God over and over. Hot meals started showing up on our doorstep every night. These meals came from church members who had all driven at least half an hour to bring them on those cold winter nights. The love that was being poured out to help us was unbelievable.

The body of Christ was working together to help me!

I began to feel my heart changing from the encouragement and the prayer that was directed toward me and my family. Satan had been right about one thing: life did go on without me, but only because of my brothers and sisters in Christ and my family, who made it go on with love. I was able to rest soundly, knowing that other families had stepped up and taken care of my family. They were being the hands and feet of Jesus.

God was using this accident in so many ways for His glory.

I kept praising and praying, and the meals kept coming. My children were being taken care of, and life was going on without me. But my faith grew, and my trust in the Lord was strengthened.

Then, God stepped in.

Jay was at work, the kids were at school, and I was still in the dark room. I lay there, my head pounding, and looked over toward Jayson's side of the bed. Tears and weakness physically broke me down.

Through a foggy mind and foggy vision, I sensed the presence of someone, and then I heard a voice. It laughed a very loud, sarcastic laugh right in my face. I wrapped the pillow around my skull and pushed, trying to get the noise to go away.

I knew it was Satan. He wanted me to go crazy!

I cried out to God. "Please make this go away!"

I grabbed my phone, squinted to see enough to turn on music, and then sat up in my bed to praise.

I sang loudly the words to the song "Homeward Bound," by Kristene DiMarco.

Finally, out of fear and frustration, I screamed, "I can't do it anymore. Please help me, God!"

I don't believe thirty seconds passed from the time I cried out to God like a crazy person, when a miracle happened right before my distorted eyes.

> In my distress I called to the Lord, and he answered me. From deep in the realm of the dead I called for help, and you listened to my cry.
> Jonah 2:2 NIV

I felt something new in the room, and I opened my eyes. It was an energy, like a white cloud forming on my wall. I shut my mouth and remained still, watching in amazement. I blinked hard and fast, watching one letter at a time appear on my wall within the cloudlike shape.

I didn't even have time to think. This happened so quickly but was so real. As the writing came together, I realized what it said.

GET UP. I'M HEALING YOU.

I sat there staring at that wall for a long time, until it faded away just as quickly as it had come. There was no one home but me. There was no way to save this moment to show anyone. God had come that close.

I felt dazed and numb. But I obeyed and slowly slid out of bed and onto my feet. I looked around, knowing I had just had an encounter with God.

I walked to the bathroom and took a shower, where I sobbed and lifted my arms to heaven with no strength to say a word, because no words would be good enough for what had just happened.

After the shower, I realized my head didn't hurt anymore at all.

I was worn out, but I had no more pain.

I was healed.

God really had come to me and healed me in that room. He met me right where I was, and although He was gentle, His words were clear, short, and simple.

Get up!

Since then, I have realized in my studies just how many times in the Bible those same words were spoken when Jesus healed someone. I get choked up and covered in goose bumps every time I read them. I could say I was amazed when I first saw the words in the Bible after this experience, but I wasn't.

I won't ever say that I expected those words and that encounter, because I know I will never be worthy of that grace and the miraculous way He came to me. But I do know Jesus. I do have a relationship with God. And I do have faith and know that God has and always will perform miracles.

Shortly after this encounter with God, I wondered how

and if I should share that story with anyone. How could I adequately explain what had happened? So I prayed about it.

For so long, I had been asking God for healing. Now I was praising Him for doing just that and asking Him what I should do next. And then God spoke to me again.

Pray to be filled with courage so that you can testify to My goodness.

After hearing from God again, I couldn't contain it. The first Sunday I was back at church leading worship, it felt like God took over my entire being. The Holy Spirit filled me. I couldn't hold in His goodness and all that He had revealed to me in that room! I had to tell them of the miracle that had happened. I praised and thanked the people of the church for being God's hands and feet, and I praised God for healing me and never leaving me alone.

But it would be much longer before I would share about the writing on the wall. I was afraid to share that part with anyone. Afraid that they would say I was crazy and that they wouldn't believe me.

I could just imagine all the thoughts:

Oh my, you were seeing things.

Well, dear, let's remember—you did have a head injury.

I know that's Satan, who likes to whisper lies in our ears.

The truth is, that head injury became a gift I could share with the world. God used it for His glory. He knew I would eventually reveal to the world that He is still in the business of performing miracles.

And, of course, if we don't believe in miracles, how will we ever identify one when it happens right before our eyes?

One night, after I had started writing this book, I was praying about what chapter to write next. I asked God to guide my thoughts and my words and to help me remember. He answered my prayers and let me know that the next chapter would be titled "The Writing on the Wall."

I scribbled down the title in the back of my journal, re-assuring myself that I would Google it. I knew that people use that phrase, but I wanted to make sure I understood the meaning.

The first thing that appeared on my Google search was a song with that title. As I kept scrolling, I realized that the phrase had originated in the book of Daniel in the Old Testament. I grabbed my NIV Bible that I had been reading through that year and literally gasped out loud when I turned to Daniel chapter five. In my Bible, the title of chapter five was "The Writing on the Wall."

Since I was on a plan to read the whole Bible in a year, I wondered if I had already read this without understanding what I was reading. I searched my calendar and confirmed that no, I had not read this story in the Bible. I was only to Jeremiah in the Old Testament. It was October, and I would not be in Daniel until December.

I immediately read the story in Daniel chapter five.

Suddenly the fingers of a human hand appeared and wrote on the plaster of the wall, near the lampstand in the royal palace. The king watched the hand as it wrote. His face turned pale, and he was so frightened that his legs became weak, and his knees were knocking.
Daniel 5:5–6 NIV

I stared at the page, yet again in complete awe at what God had done. Affirmation that I was not crazy. God writes on walls. All that happens now has happened before and will happen again.

God doesn't change; He changes us.

Chapter Fourteen

Forgiveness

Having a direct encounter with God changes things.

After the experience in my bedroom, there was no doubt that He deserved my everything, and this includes my absolute obedience to His Word. My desire to be obedient to God was growing more and more. I had not let my past go completely, nor had I forgiven my dad for the pain he caused me as a child. But I was learning that I *should* forgive him.

I couldn't be free until I really forgave, but I just didn't know how that was possible. I didn't have the power to fix my heart and erase the scars. I started to question myself.

Had I forgiven him?

Was it possible to forgive someone you could never reconcile with face-to-face?

It had taken me years to realize that my dad's death was what had first led me to Christ. If someone asked, I would say that I had forgiven my dad and felt sad that he was gone. But the hurtful memories hadn't gone away, and the pain was still the same every time I remembered.

I was beginning to figure out that holding on to this unforgiveness was only hurting me. The fact that I hadn't truly forgiven my dad was internal torture.

And then one Sunday, our friend Kenny preached on Matthew 18:32–35.

Then the master called the servant in. "You wicked servant," he said. "I canceled all that debt of yours because you begged me to. Shouldn't you have had mercy on your fellow servant just as I had on you?" In anger his master handed him over to the jailers to be tortured, until he should pay back all that he owed. This is how my heavenly Father will treat each of you unless you forgive your brother or sister from your heart. Matthew 18:32–35 NIV

Kenny explained Jesus's parable this way: The torture we would experience wouldn't be from people torturing us physically, but torture within. When we harbor unforgiveness, we relive the hurt, but that only tortures us, not the person who caused us pain.

This was especially true in a case like mine, where the person I had not forgiven was dead and had been for years. He couldn't hurt me anymore, yet I was living like he could.

Kenny explained that when we do this, we're actually looking past everything God did for us by sending His one and only Son, Jesus Christ, to die for us on the cross. Jesus has already suffered for us. He's already paid the price for our sin, and unforgiveness is a sin. I was continuing to sin every day that I didn't forgive my dad. I was looking completely past the remarkable pain that Jesus endured for me.

It sounds silly, but I ran to Google for this question too. After typing in "How do you know if you've really forgiven someone?" I found an article entitled "John Piper Offers Four Suggestions for Those Struggling to Forgive, Reveals 'Real Sign' of Forgiveness." It says, "The real sign of forgiveness is that you don't seek to punish the other, you seek the good of the other."[2]

I felt this to be true in my heart. I had obviously been concerned about where my dad had gone. I didn't want any harm to be done to him. But I still found it hard sometimes to be sure I had forgiven him, because I still held on to so much hurt.

I began to pray that God would help me know for sure if I had forgiven my dad. I wanted to truly forgive him, but I didn't understand the process. I desired to be obedient to scripture and do the right thing in the eyes of the Lord.

God answered my prayer.

I walked into church one Sunday, recognizing all the familiar faces. We were shaking hands and basking in the glory of the fellowship that had become so special at Olive Tree.

As the greetings were about to end, I began making my way to the platform.

Unexpectedly, a gentleman put his hand on my shoulder and said, "Good morning, young lady."

This man was a stranger to me, but his presence instantly shook me to my core. He was a big man in frame and stature.

---

2 Leah MarieAnn Klett, "John Piper Offers 4 Suggestions for Those Struggling to Forgive: Reveals 'Real Sign' of Forgiveness," *The Christian Post*, accessed January 24, 2022, https://www.christianpost.com/news/john-piper-offers-4-suggestions-struggling-to-forgive-reveals-sign-of-forgiveness.html.

His hands were large and his eyes kind. His body language put me in the mindset of someone very familiar, making me question if I *did* know him from somewhere.

Then it dawned on me. He reminded me of my dad. I couldn't help but stare. His hand on my shoulder had felt like my dad's hand.

Emotions welled up as I stood on the platform. I couldn't stop stealing quick glances at the gentleman out of the corner of my eye.

Worship was exceptionally emotional that day.

Kenny brought his message and tugged at hearts in all the most wonderful ways.

And then we took communion, which isn't a routine thing in this church. Kenny always mentioned before communion that if you hadn't been saved or you had a heart issue with someone or if something just wasn't right with another person, you should reconsider partaking in communion until the issue was resolved.

Therefore, if you are offering your gift at the altar and there remember that your brother or sister has something against you, leave your gift there in front of the altar. First go and be reconciled to them; then come and offer your gift.
Matthew 5:23–24 NIV

I felt convicted because I didn't know for sure that I had forgiven my dad. I bowed my head and began to pray. *Lord, I don't want to be that person who does not take communion because of a hardened heart. But I don't want to be disobedient and take it, not knowing for sure if I have forgiven my dad.*

Then another miracle happened! The tears started flowing from my eyes as I remembered our drive to church that morning.

Jayson, Savannah, and Noah had all been talking about the dreams they'd had the night before. They were happy dreams that made for good conversation and laughs. I knew that I'd had a dream as well, but I couldn't remember it. It felt like it was an important one that I should remember, but I just couldn't. I'd been frustrated that I couldn't contribute my dream to the conversation, but it would not come to me.

Now, as I sat there in church, my head bowed in prayer, I remembered my dream.

In the dream, I had been in a room with a lot of people I didn't recognize. It was a very bright room, and the people were organized in what seemed to be a large choir. They were all wearing white, and there was a glow illuminating the group. I'd been standing right in front of all the people as if I were the director of the choir.

As I conducted the choir, my eyes met with one of the individuals singing. I knew that I knew this person but felt awkward making eye contact. I kept looking away, trying not to stare, but in a room of what seemed like thousands of people, my eyes connected with this one individual over and over. Then I realized.

It was my dad.

He looked good. He didn't have his glasses on anymore. He wasn't overweight. He was a younger version of the man I had known.

He didn't say anything to me in that dream. He only smiled and continued singing in the choir. But he didn't need to say anything; his smile said it all, and I'd smiled back.

I began squirming with excitement in that pew as it sank in what had just happened. That was it—that was my dream! The man I had made eye contact with was my dad, and he was in heaven, happy and at peace.

At this point, my body was shaking, and the tears were pouring. God had revealed this dream to me as I prayed.

I truly believe that the stranger, who I would later learn is named Mike, was sent to jar my memory that morning.

God spoke to me in that moment and said, *I have forgiven your dad. If you know that I have forgiven, how could you not? You get up and partake in communion and be at peace.*

My heart has been changed ever since.

This peace has not left me. I have not needed to question my forgiveness for my dad since. It was a sealed deal—over, finished. Jesus took it because He loves me, and I let Him. God allowed me to move on from my past, and that has allowed me to continue to grow in Christ.

Our God is a great big God, my friends. I had never before, in all my life, felt the relief and peace that I found in that moment. I had unknowingly carried that hurt for so long.

The only thing that changed my heart and gave me peace was prayer.

Lord, please let me never forget that You used dreams in the Old and the New Testament to speak to Your people, and even more than that, You are the same yesterday and today and forever.

If God spoke through dreams in biblical times, why would He not speak through dreams now? Amen!

The crazy thing is Mike has become like a grandparent to my children. He has been at church every Sunday since then, and now his whole family is there with him. He has invited us to his house and regularly brings gifts to Savannah and Noah. He has filled a role that my dad should have had in their lives, and I am so thankful for him and the way that God orchestrated that whole occurrence.

On June 1, 2019, Mike came to know the Lord and was saved. On August 4, 2019, we had a baptism service at Olive

Tree where my mom, Mark, Mike, and I were all immersed as an act of obedience and public display that we had all given our lives to the Lord.

What blows my mind is that God had this planned all along. He knew my dad would pass. He knew I would struggle. He knew that fourteen years later, I would have that dream. He specifically put Mike there to jolt my memory and remind me of my dad. He filled that space that had been empty for so long.

I learned about forgiveness. I learned that mistakes will be made. Sometimes huge mistakes. I learned that hurt will be in every one of our lives. But what comes when we pray for God to help us forgive someone is far greater and more fulfilling than holding a grudge.

If you're having trouble finding a way to forgive someone, I encourage you to give it to the Lord. He promises to help you.

I can testify that when I was set free from bitterness and unforgiveness, my life got better. I can't believe the peace I feel sometimes when I start to remember my dad and the old memories that I carried with me. I now feel love and forgiveness, and that can only come from Jesus.

> Forgive and you will be forgiven.
> Luke 6:37 NIV.

I learned that I never really hated my dad. I hated the alcohol, I hated the drugs, and I hated the demons living within him. But I loved the man that God had created. I loved my dad.

We forgive because He first forgave us.

C. S. Lewis once said, "To be a Christian means to forgive the inexcusable because God has forgiven the inexcusable in you."

My biggest lesson in forgiveness was that I learned to erase the hurt, not the people, because as the scripture says, the battle is not against flesh and blood (Ephesians 6:12). I remind myself often that I am to walk with a forgiving heart, ready to forgive before anything even happens, because I desire to be obedient to the scriptures and to grow more and more like Jesus.

Chapter Fifteen

Going Home

On October 5, 2020, the fifteenth anniversary of my dad's death, I got the urge to call a photographer. I was about halfway through the first draft of this manuscript, but I was beginning to wonder if I would ever finish.

So, like I'm sure all professional writers do, I set up a photoshoot for the cover of the book. I thought, *If I can imagine what the cover will look like, that means I can imagine it being real and done.*

It was again fall in Ohio, and the leaves were picturesque. I decided I wanted to capture the change in the seasons before the storms came and muddied it all up, like they always do. So I called a photographer who had been recommended to me by the only other person I knew who had written a book. The photographer's name is Annie. She had one session left for the month, and that was the very next day.

That date was October 6. My dad's birthday! It would have been his sixtieth.

I saw this as a sign and took the session.

As I hung up the phone, I panicked a little. I was not prepared for a photoshoot! I had no idea what to wear or where to go. I collected my keys and wallet, then announced to the kids that we needed to hurry and get in the car.

Before they could ask a thousand questions about where we were going and why, I eagerly explained that I needed to find a background for my book cover, because I had set up a photoshoot for the next day.

They were not thrilled about pulling themselves off the comfortable couch and acted annoyed as we rushed to the car. I begged them to just enjoy the ride and let me focus. They responded with eyerolls but obeyed. Relieved, I drew in a deep breath. I didn't have the energy to explain any more to them.

Fighting a bout of panic, I pulled out of the driveway and decided to search for the most beautifully colored trees I could find.

I drove to a town thirty minutes away and pulled into a nature center. I asked the kids to stay put for a minute while I got out of the car. I looked up, admiring the beauty that the trees held. I turned in slow circles, noticing that the paths had been freshly mowed and manicured and that some of the leaves from the giant trees along the paths were hanging close enough to touch. Around me, one beautifully colored leaf at a time drifted down, and I tried to picture the cover. This place was beyond beautiful, but it didn't feel right.

I hopped back into the car and hurried down the road, trying to beat the sunset. I pulled onto the campus of the college I had once attended. This was where I'd received the emergency phone call about my dad.

The college was set back off the road, situated in the middle of a forest of colors. Memories of walking those sidewalks surfaced, and I remembered the sound of the leaves crunching beneath my shoes. This location was beautiful as well.

I looked around, trying to find the perfect spot, imagining again what my cover would look like. And then it hit me. How could I not have thought of this sooner? It might not offer the most beautiful scenery, but I knew exactly where I needed to go.

I rushed back to the car and drove for another ten minutes, watching as the sun sank lower and lower.

We arrived at my destination, and I was relieved to see that there were trees changing color there too, as I had hoped.

But even more important, there was my story. This was where I grew up. The house where so much had happened. The house where it all began.

I pulled up to the curb and put the car in park. Looking out the window, I saw the little hill on the sidewalk that I used to think was so big but really was just the size of an ant hill. The house had been beautifully landscaped and painted since we lived there, but our mailbox still hung untouched with the number sixteen and an Amish buggy picture beside it. That mailbox, where Josh and I had placed our letters to Santa. The same box that my mom's and dad's hands had reached in to gather all the Christmas cards that were received each year.

There was still no front porch. Only a few cement steps to enter the house. Those steps that my brother had flown down in pure horror when he found our dad that October day. Those steps that they wheeled my dad's body down when they took him away from the house forever.

I couldn't help but turn my focus to the window of the bedroom where he had lain lifeless. I imagined all the cars and people who passed by that day, no one knowing he lay in there dead.

Savannah and Noah didn't say a word; they just stared at the house. They knew about this place. I had told them the stories. They let me take it all in.

I made my way down to the park that you could see from the front steps.

The same playground equipment was there, but it had been cleaned up and painted. I got out of the car with the kids following me. As they ran to play on the old wooden teeter-totters, I headed for my swing. The same swing where I had taken refuge so many times. Where I would pump out my anger until I could almost reach the sky.

I fitted myself into the seat and pushed off with my toes. I felt the wind that used to dry my tears hit my now-smiling face, and the familiar tickle in my stomach that would always make me giggle. I closed my eyes just as I had as a child when I would let the wind blow my problems away and thanked God for the opportunity to come back to this place, *changed.*

As I looked around, I knew this was where the photoshoot should be.

That night, I sent Annie the chapter describing my dad's death. I'll admit that was a scary move, since I had not edited it at all, and I had never written a book before. But I wanted her to know why we were there and what I was trying to accomplish with this session.

The next day, Annie and I stood in the park, admiring all the beautiful trees.

After taking in the scenery, she said, "Okay, where do you want to start?"

With my Bible in hand, I said, "Let's start on the swing."

Sitting there, I smiled for the camera, then looked down at the Word. *Thank You, God, for the life I'm living now, compared to the life I was living then.*

Changed.

When we were done on the swing, Annie asked where I would like to go next. I told her there was a big rock at the corner of the park where I used to sit as a child, claiming it as my own in the neighborhood. I called it my "thinking rock."

At the rock, I ran my fingers over the top, remembering the familiar grooves that remained unchanged.

After several shots of me on the rock, I told Annie that I had brought my dad's pocket watch with me. I felt it was fitting, since it was the only thing that I had kept of his. She directed me to sit in the leaves and hold the watch as I stared down at it.

I took a deep breath and thanked God again that I had been able to see through the eyes of Jesus and finally forgive my dad. I could be at the park and hold his pocket watch without regretful tears. I could finally, after all this time, smile, knowing that all was well with my soul and with his.

Change.

When we were done with this pose, we started walking away from the park, toward my old house. Annie with her beautiful leather camera bag, me with my hipster leather bookbag, like we were famous foreigners.

I hadn't recognized anyone yet, except my old neighbor. The one who had been doing the dishes the day my dad passed away. I noticed her walking into her house as we made our way in that direction.

As we neared my childhood home, Annie said, "Let's go knock on the door and see if it's okay for you to sit on the steps and get some shots."

I smiled a smile that said, of course we could do that. But really, I felt butterflies crashing into each other in my stomach.

To her, this was an obvious background.

To me, this was an emotional milestone.

I felt brave though, and by now so many people had come out of their houses to see what was going on with the famous foreigners that I began playing the part. I held my head high and walked right up that huge ant hill, then on up the cement steps, and knocked on the door.

A little boy answered, his mom hurrying behind him, carrying a baby on one arm and a bottle in the other hand.

I smiled and said hello, trying as hard as I could to see around her without looking rude or dangerous. I explained that I had grown up in this house and asked if it would be okay if we took some pictures outside on the steps for a project I was working on.

She didn't seem too interested, as she was busy tending to her children. She smiled and simply said, "Sure. I'll shut the door so you can get this pretty fall wreath in your pictures."

She had no idea what stories hid in those walls.

Why did I want to go inside that house so badly? What did I think I would find?

I tucked in my emotions and played the part. I was the explorer. Annie was the photographer. I was back in history, remembering, while she captured the story through her lens.

I looked back at the mailbox. *Snap.*

I looked up at the sky. *Snap.*

I looked out in the direction of my thinking rock. *Snap.*

I looked down to the park. *Snap, snap.*

Then I stood up, looked one more time at the front door. No *snap.* I looked down. No *snap.* And I thanked God that I had gotten through this day, without anger and without tears.

Change.

We began walking back to the park, and Annie snapped more pictures. Looking right, I saw my old house. Looking left, I saw my rock and pictured the broken little girl who used to sit there. Looking forward, I saw the swing.

Looking back. I imagined them taking my dad away.

Looking up, I thanked God for bringing me back here, to deal with the emotions that had been left untouched for far too long. I had run from my problems. I had run from my hurts. I'd run far and searched hard to fill the void that I'd felt when I drove away from that house years ago.

But it wasn't until I ran to the Father that He began to show me:

It's time. It's time to go home and deal with what was always yours. Your story. It's time to forget all the hurt and realize that there was always good in those moments as well. It's time to learn. It's time to grow, and it's time to smile when you drive down these roads.

It's time to accept the change and realize that everything that happened brought you to Me.

It's time to bring your children here and make new memories. Time to let them feel a piece of their mother as a child.

There will always be pain. There will always be storms that muddy up the beauty, but dear Lord, please don't ever let me forget that the beauty is always there if we look for it, and those big problems that seem like mountains are indeed only ant hills to You.

Chapter Sixteen

My Prayer for You

When God came to me in the dream telling me it was time to write the book, I didn't know why, I just knew that I had to be obedient. But as God revealed His will little by little for this project, I grew more and more amazed at His creativity. He urged me to create in order to help me understand Him and the gospel. I sat at my dining room table, hour upon hour, for two years putting the pieces of my life together, trying so hard to remember and capture everywhere I had seen God.

The process of working through those past hurts, regrets, memories, and lessons helped me to see that my past was of no importance anymore, because that had been my life before I was saved and born again.

I realized that I am new!

> Therefore, if anyone is in Christ, he is a new creation; old things have passed away; behold all things have become new.
> 2 Corinthians 5:17 NKJV

I realized I was living the gospel of victory in my own life. The new me had been forming; and the parts I was holding on to, even the sadness and hurt that wanted to keep creeping back in, had no place in my new identity.

I had been one way until I allowed Jesus into my life to save me, then I had repented and turned—there's no going back. The circumstances that I had lived had made me believe I was unworthy of love and peace in my life. But when I prayed that prayer during the thunderstorm, not understanding what I was doing but being guided by Jesus, everything began to change.

I slowly started to understand that God had sent His Son, Jesus, to hang on the cross to be crucified, to save me and you.

The salvation I received—the same salvation God desires for you—grants us a place in heaven for eternal life. That is an amazing part of the gift.

The gift of salvation is also meant for peace and understanding while we're on earth. I see now that while I'm still in this body, the biggest gift of salvation is my relationship with God, Jesus, and the Holy Spirit—three in one!

I pray to the Father now because I know He's there and He hears me.

I praise Jesus because I realize the sacrifice He made to save a wretch like me.

And I cherish my relationship with the Holy Spirit, the Spirit of God living within me, because I feel Him in my heartbeats and I hear Him whisper in my ear.

Jesus hung on that cross to restore what God intended you and me to be in the first place.

His.

The problems I faced in my life were real, and the hurt that came with them was hard. How can I discredit what God did for me, knowing the truth? How can I live like Jesus's death wasn't enough, like Jesus wasn't enough, and live like my salvation is not sufficient to transform me? Knowing the truth, I can no longer lean on or go back to any part of my past self. If I held on to the past, I wouldn't be living out the gospel. I wouldn't be accepting the gift of newness.

I lean into Jesus's arms, because He is enough.

I'm saved.

I'm truly saved.

I can rest under His wings because I am a child of God.

I have Christ inside of me, who is the Holy Spirit, who is GOD!

> For the Son of Man came to seek and to save the lost.
> Luke 19:10 NIV

I'm now able to lay down my past, along with a finished book, at the feet of Jesus, where it was always meant to be.

Jesus transformed my life, and His desire is to do the same for you.

My prayer for you is that you come to know God as more than an image or idea that people acknowledge but still feel distant from. I pray you read the Bible, the true Word, and let it speak to you the way God intends you to perceive it through the Holy Spirit. I assure you, you will find peace and comfort in the pages that have always been waiting for you.

What is the gospel?

If you are like I once was and don't understand salvation, rest assured, it's not as far off as you think. To be saved means you were going your own way, which leads to death—there is a way *that seems* right to a man, but its end *is* the way of death

(Proverbs 14:12 NKJV)—but you have repented (acknowledged and confessed your sin) and turned toward God for help. You repent by admitting you are a sinner, which we all are.

> If you confess with your mouth the Lord Jesus and believe in your heart that God has raised Him from the dead, you will be saved. For with the heart one believes unto righteousness, and with the mouth confession is made unto salvation. Romans 10:9–10 NKJV

The gospel is all about love. God sending His Son to save us was great love. Jesus's willingness to endure the agony of the cross and lay down His life for our good was great love. Jesus's rising from the dead not only proves the power and love of God, but it gives us a clear example that we, too, can rise above our old selves through the power of Jesus Christ. We can die to our flesh and be raised in the spirit that God gives us.

I can look in the mirror now and see nothing but love. Those angry eyes don't look back at me anymore. The eyes of God's Spirit live within me now, and they are the eyes of peace. There is meaning in my story and in where God brought me from. All the experiences are dear to me and remind me of God's gentleness and power. But the ultimate meaning is Jesus.

Jesus saves, and He loves us.

Acknowledgments

Jayson. Wow, what a journey this has been. Who would have ever guessed our music would take us from the bars to the church? No one! *But God.* The lessons we've experienced together have not always been easy, but I'm so thankful for each one and that God has brought us through them together, stronger.

Jay, you are an amazing husband and an even more amazing dad to our children. Thank you for that, and thank you for always encouraging me in everything I do. There is no way I could have ever had the confidence I needed to write a book without a little bit of the dreamer in you wearing off on me. What a wonderful peace it gives me to know that no matter what happens the rest of our days on earth, we will be worshipping the Lord together forever in heaven. I love you!

Savannah, where do I begin? You are so far beyond your years, and I am so proud of you and who you are becoming. You are the definition of patience and self-control, and I admire you for that. I'm sorry you had to be dragged along with us your first few years before we knew Jesus, but I'm also thankful you got to see and experience God's work in your parents as it unfolded. I pray peace over you, Savannah Love, and that you would seek God all the days of your life and lean on Jesus in every situation. Sweet, sophisticated Savannah, you are a gem. Don't ever forget that. I love you!

Noah-Boah, when I think of you, I think of joy. I pray you remain as joyful as you are right now, all the days of your life. You have never met a stranger, and I love that about you. I pray you use that gift to minister to others and share the gospel. Your confidence, wisdom, and quick wit inspire me. I am so proud of you. I pray peace over you, Noah Jay, and that you would seek God all the days of your life and lean on Jesus in every situation. Noah, please keep the laughter alive while you're here on earth, and keep that confidence to praise Jesus, lifting your arms no matter where you are or who's watching. I love you!

Josh. My prayer for you is that you know you are loved by the most high God! I pray you can find unexplainable peace on this earth so that you can experience the full joy that the Father intends for each one of His children. I pray that you, too, can move on from the life we once knew and never again be reminded of the darkness that lived there with us, but only see God, and Jesus, for who He is and rest there. I love you, brother.

Mom. I pray you see the peace in the pages of this book and understand how much I love you. I'm so grateful that I got to witness your journey to find the Lord firsthand. I know I tried to capture a lot of our story in these pages, but only you and I will ever fully know the intensity of that life and what God brought us from. What a gift we share. I pray you know how much you are loved and that you remember to *lean back* all the days of your life. God's got you, and Jesus is enough. Love you!

Mark. You and I have never talked about the past or about the season in which you entered my life. It was a rough season, but I pray you see that was the turning point when everything started to get better in our family. God works in mysterious ways, and the fact that our relationship started by you offering to carry my baggage is no coincidence. I'm glad we were able to share in the experience of baptism that summer day in 2019, when we were both able to lay it all down and leave the baggage in that pond. I love you, Mark, but I will never let you win at Ping-Pong.

Mamaw. You're everything to me. Although Jesus is my ultimate Savior, you're next. There is no way I could ever thank you enough for everything you have done for me over the years. You have consistently been *you* and the only solid in my life when things were rocky.

When I think of you, I think of that kitchen table where we had so many conversations. But the conversation that tops them all happened while I was writing this book, when I realized that you and I had never talked about your salvation. It hit me like a ton of bricks as I stood in my kitchen doing dishes one evening, and I had to know if my mamaw knew Jesus. When I rushed to your house and we settled in at the table, you eased so much in my heart, answering my question. I felt like a fool asking someone so wise if they knew Jesus, but your gentle "yes" was a lullaby to my soul. I love you!

Kenny and Kim. I can't even imagine life not knowing you two. Thank you for sharing in our excitement to finish this book. Thank you for loving God and for being obedient to the Word. Thank you for praying for not only a lead worshipper but for their family to come to the church long before you even knew us. And thank you for sharing your journal entry that showed us how long those prayers were being prayed before we came. Prayer is so powerful!

Most of all, thank you for encouraging, teaching, and loving my family and the flock at Olive Tree. This journey with you two has obviously been orchestrated by God, and it's such a beautiful relationship. Thank you both for being faithful and modeling Jesus well. I love you both!

Steph. Thank you for being my biggest encourager throughout the writing of this book. You are so special to me and have been such a huge part of my journey. I never dreamed a neighbor could be so obviously sent by God. It has been such a blessing to walk with you in our journey to know Christ more intimately. You will never know how much I needed you all those times you showed up on my porch, coffee in hand. I must admit, I have always seen you as a Mary and me as a Martha. Driving home and seeing you on your front porch, indulging in the Word, does something to my heart and frequently reminds me to slow down myself. I am so thankful for our friendship and sisterhood. Love you, neighbor!

Laura (graphic designer) and Annie (photographer). What a blessing to work with you both on this project! The fact that I could share this experience with other faithful believers is beyond a blessing. I feel so close to you both and appreciate everything you did to make sure the cover was not only beautiful but told a story in itself. I am forever grateful and love you both!

Lesley. Last but certainly of utmost importance, Lesley! The idea of having my first book edited by someone who is so experienced in the writing world was a bit scary. The actual experience was exciting, humbling, and more fun than I ever imagined. There is no doubt that meeting you was a blessing from God. I am blown away by your knowledge, your patience, your gentleness, and your overall talent. I always thought I understood what an editor did. I was wrong! But it felt like you were a friend from the beginning of the process, and you made this so enjoyable. I thank you and appreciate your kind spirit and positive attitude throughout this process. I'm excited to see what's in store for the future. Love you, Lesley! Oh, and I will be using the word "boon" a lot more, now that I know it exists without the "e."

I wish I had all the space to list everyone who was important to me in this book, but that's not realistic. I have been blessed with too many wonderful relationships.

If I haven't mentioned you, you know who you are.

Old friend, new friend, Olive Tree family, MCS family, UMC family, reader I've never met . . . I love you, and more importantly, God loves you! I pray the one thing you take away from my story is that God is patient and that He desires that you come to Him with everything and grow in a relationship with Him, no matter your past. I pray that as you close this book, the next book you open is a Bible.

I pray the wonder has just begun for those of you who never knew the truth.

We can all be changed, but it's God who changes us.

All glory to God.

ORDER INFORMATION

REDEMPTION
P R E S S

To order additional copies of this book, please visit
www.redemption-press.com.
Also available at Christian bookstores and Barnes and Noble.

CPSIA information can be obtained
at www.ICGtesting.com
Printed in the USA
BVHW042205100922
646749BV00005B/258